Additional Praise for *The NASCAR Way*

"DuPont has been involved in many sports marketing programs, but our association with Rick Henrick, Jeff Gordon, and NASCAR has been, by far, the most rewarding. Our customers and employees are deeply involved and enormously motivated by all aspects of our NASCAR association."

> —Edgar S. Woolard, Jr.
> Chairman
> DuPont

"The history of NASCAR is a tremendous success story, complete with heroes, drama, courage, and characters. We are proud to be part of the story that *The NASCAR Way* captures and chronicles."

> —John Wildhack
> Senior Vice President, Programming
> ESPN

"*The NASCAR Way* is very interesting. There's a wealth of information here: a good mix of NASCAR's history along with current information."

> —Torrey Galida
> Manager
> Ford Global Motorsport Marketing

"It is remarkable that 50 years of good, sound business by a very focused family has resulted in *The NASCAR Way*. Robert Hagstrom writes about how this sport is an opportunity for entertainment, marketing, and investing all in one package: NASCAR."

> —Don Hawk
> President
> Dale Earnhardt, Inc.

"A rare and accurate look inside the business of stock car racing—thorough and well presented."

> —John E. Graham, Jr.
> President
> Daytona International Speedway

"Robert Hagstrom has done a remarkable job of providing successful marketing strategies to the reader about NASCAR racing and the reasons why race team sponsorships sell products. He has woven an interesting and colorful racing history into a business-related chronicle."

—Ben White
Managing Editor
NASCAR Winston Cup Illustrated

"Robert Hagstrom's insights and observations about NASCAR and its business practices keep the reader's attention from start to finish—just like one of our races!"

—Jim Hunter
President
Darlington Raceway

"Thanks, Robert, for taking me back to the Waldorf in November, 1996. Your vivid description of Rick Hendrick entering the ballroom brought a tear to my eye, but at the same time recaptured one of the great moments of my life."

—Jimmy Johnson
Vice President and General Manager
Hendrick Motorsports

The NASCAR Way

The NASCAR Way

The Business That Drives the Sport

Robert G. Hagstrom

John Wiley & Sons, Inc.

New York • Chichester • Weinheim • Brisbane • Singapore • Toronto

This text is printed on acid-free paper.

Copyright © 1998 by Robert G. Hagstrom.
Published by John Wiley & Sons, Inc.

All rights reserved. Published simultaneously in Canada.

Reproduction or translation of any part of this work beyond
that permitted by Section 107 or 108 of the 1976 United
States Copyright Act without the permission of the copyright
owner is unlawful. Requests for permission or further
information should be addressed to the Permissions Department,
John Wiley & Sons, Inc.

This publication is designed to provide accurate and authoritative
information in regard to the subject matter covered. It is sold
with the understanding that the publisher is not engaged in
rendering legal, accounting, or other professional services. If
legal advice or other expert assistance is required, the services
of a competent professional person should be sought.

Library of Congress Cataloging in Publication Data:

Hagstrom, Robert G., 1956–
    The NASCAR way : the business that drives the sport / Robert G.
Hagstrom.
        p.   cm.
    Includes index.
    ISBN 0-471-18316-4 (cloth : alk. paper)
    1. NASCAR (Association)   2. NASCAR (Association)—Finance.
3. Stock car racing—United States.   4. Stock car racing—Economic
aspects—United States.   I. Title.
GV1029.9.S74H34   1998
796.72'0973–dc21   97-37082

Printed in the United States of America

10 9 8 7 6 5 4 3 2 1

Lovingly dedicated to Kim, Robert, and John, who never fail to keep their dad entertained.

FOREWORD

When Robert Hagstrom first approached us about doing a foreword for this book, my initial reaction was to pass. I've got a full plate without spending any time on a foreword for a business book on racing.

We were told Hagstrom had put together a pretty interesting overview of how NASCAR works. What makes us tick. It's a look at our sport from the business side. Hagstrom looks at NASCAR as a sanctioning association, he looks at the tracks as NASCAR's stadiums, the athletes (drivers) as our stars, the car owners and sponsors as our marketing partners, and he does it in a way that captures the overall "one big family" atmosphere that makes NASCAR racing such a unique professional sport. He also looks at the most important ingredient in NASCAR's business today: our fans, a cultural cross-section of Americans whose loyalty to NASCAR sponsors is unmatched in professional sports today.

My father (William H. G. "Big Bill" France) taught me long ago that hard work is the real foundation of any successful venture. With that in mind, I have bumped into Hagstrom everywhere I've been over the last two years: in the tracks' garages, in the corporate hospitality suites, in the pits, at our corporate offices, during our annual NASCAR Winston Cup Series Awards Banquet at the Waldorf-Astoria in New York, in the car haulers talking to drivers, in business offices talking to track owners, virtually everywhere.

NASCAR racing is a very complex business that requires solid business techniques and modern-day creative marketing plans. There's no magic, no tricks. It's really about hard work, and creating an environment where everybody wins.

Hagstrom's insights and observations bring a refreshing "outside" business perspective to our industry. We're glad he took the time to do it. We might learn something from it. That's the nature of our business. Learning something every day is truly the NASCAR Way.

William C. France
President, NASCAR

Daytona Beach, Florida
October 1997

PREFACE

I DID NOT come to NASCAR, the National Association for Stock Car Auto Racing, by one of the interstate routes that lead to its famous tracks. Millions of fans have reached NASCAR over the past several years by either attending a race or watching the sport on television. But my pathway was unique. I first came to NASCAR by reading an income statement and balance sheet, and what I saw was every bit as exciting as watching stock cars race at 190 miles an hour.

Soon after writing *The Warren Buffett Way* (Wiley, 1994), I had the opportunity to develop a new no-load mutual fund called Focus Trust. In my role as its portfolio manager, I look for companies that fit the investment parameters outlined in the Buffett book. My analysis has always included an evaluation of a company's business, management, and financial tenets.

First, I look for companies that are simple and understandable and have a consistent operating history. Second, for a company to succeed, it must have a management team that is honest and candid and forever works to rationally allocate the capital of the business.

Third, the most valuable companies tend to generate a high return on invested capital and consistently produce cash earnings for their shareholders.

One of the first purchases by Focus Trust was a company called International Speedway Corporation (ISCB-OTC). International Speedway owns racetracks, including Daytona International Speedway, Talladega Superspeedway, and Darlington Raceway.

Using the methodology outlined in *The Warren Buffett Way*, it was very easy to see that International Speedway fit all of the investment tenets. Running a racetrack is a very simple and understandable business, and because the company has managed racetracks since 1949, there was a very detailed operating history to analyze.

The financial analysis of International Speedway revealed outstanding economics. The company has consistently been able to generate above-average returns on capital and significant cash earnings for shareholders.

The France family, led by Bill France, Jr., and Jim France, who own 60 percent of the outstanding stock, are known to be outstanding managers who have no trouble rationally allocating the resources of the company.

Looking backward, it was easy to see how International Speedway fit so neatly with all of the necessary investment tenets. But it was looking forward that triggered in me a deep sense of excitement. It quickly became clear that International Speedway stands to benefit directly from the robust economics of our country's largest and fastest-growing spectator sport.

To fully understand International Speedway, I first had to learn about NASCAR, the racing organization that sanctions races for twelve different divisions, including the popular Winston Cup series, the most competitive and popular form of stock car racing in the country. International Speedway, in turn, receives over 80 percent of its revenues from NASCAR-sanctioned races, with the largest contribution coming from the Winston Cup series.

An educated guess about the value of International Speedway requires a detailed understanding of NASCAR. I knew I had to do some homework.

Over the years, many good books have been written about the sport of stock car racing, but none has probed the business of this sport. I set about to investigate the phenomenon called stock car racing and the business model that propels it.

What I found was eye-popping. It wasn't the obvious that overwhelmed me. I already knew that NASCAR Winston Cup races regularly house 150,000 race fans each weekend, and I was aware that television ratings place stock car racing second only to the National Football League. What I didn't know about was the intricate financial relationships that connect NASCAR with leading U.S. corporations, with drivers who are among the highest paid athletes in the country, and with millions of weekly racegoers. My research and interviews taught me that:

- Seventy of the Fortune 500 corporations are actively involved in NASCAR.
- NASCAR has become the most hotly sought property for media broadcast rights.
- The direct benefits of sponsorship-based marketing are in the seven- to ten-figure range.
- Top stock car drivers can make millions of dollars each year—not from racing, but from marketing—because they have a singular competitive advantage.

If you come to stock car racing with some unflattering preconceptions about the sport and the people who love it, the facts about the sport today will make you put those prejudices aside. You will find, as I did, that the world of NASCAR is rich with valuable business lessons. My purpose here has been to capture those lessons and, so that your ride is more enjoyable, to share some of the excitement inherent in this superb, uniquely American sport.

If you are looking for a lesson in sponsorship-based marketing,

If you want to uncover the investment opportunities available in NASCAR,

If you want to observe the management skills of a three-generation family business,

If you want to learn about the most successful business model in sports entertainment,

Welcome to The NASCAR Way.

ROBERT G. HAGSTROM

Wayne, Pennsylvania
November 1997

ACKNOWLEDGMENTS

WHEN YOU START down a new road in life, people who are familiar with the path and who are willing to share what they know can be invaluable. I consider myself very fortunate that so many knowledgeable and generous people helped me understand "The NASCAR Way."

First and foremost, I owe a great deal of thanks to the France family for allowing me the opportunity to understand this business model. Brian France opened the door and introduced me to his father, Bill France, Jr.; his uncle, Jim France; and his sister, Lesa France Kennedy. Writing this book was all the more pleasurable because of the kindness shown to me by this exceptional family.

The greater NASCAR family is a unique enterprise that includes the staff of the NASCAR organization, track owners, team owners and members, drivers, corporate sponsors, and media representatives. In all my years as a business analyst, I have never interacted with so many courteous and professional people.

A special thanks to Paul Brooks, director of special projects and publications at NASCAR, who was my liaison and never turned down a request, and to Lisa Frandsen, Paul's assistant, who helped keep return phone calls to a minimum.

Also at NASCAR I wish to thank John Griffin, Blake Davidson, David Hyatt, Susan Moss, Doug Fritz, Judy Haydt, George Pyne, Steve Schiffman, Mike Helton, Gary Nelson, and Kevin Triplett.

If you are looking for the best in southern hospitality, the model is Darlington Raceway. Jim Hunter, its president, was invaluable to this project. He taught me much and treated me royally, not once but twice. Thank you, Jim. Thanks also to Bridget Blackwell, Russell Branham, Mac Josey, Pat Howle, and Harold King, Darlington's elder statesman and official ambassador.

John Graham, president of Daytona International Speedway, and Humpy Wheeler, president of Charlotte Motor Speedway, spent many hours teaching me the business of running a track. Thank you both.

I learned why corporate America has taken such a keen interest in NASCAR by talking with Bill Schmidt and Ed Shull at Gatorade, David Paro at McDonald's, Michael Hargrave and Marc Abel at Anheuser-Busch, Tim Garner at Garner & Nevins, Ed Stonich and Bob Yearick at DuPont, Kevin Kennedy at Ford Motor Company, and T. Wayne Robertson at R.J. Reynolds' Sports Marketing Enterprise.

Several media representatives graciously spent their time educating me. I am particularly grateful to Neal Pilson at Pilson Communications, who helped me understand the role of television in NASCAR, and to Barbara Zidovsky, vice president at Nielsen Media Research, who supplied and analyzed countless pages of television results. Thanks also to John Wildhack at ESPN and David Hall at TNN. A special thanks to John McMullin at MRN, who explained the radio component in NASCAR, and to Wayne Harris at WNPC-FM and Chris Wallace at WDOV-AM radio.

The reporters and journalists who cover NASCAR are a special breed. I am indebted to Ben White at *NASCAR Winston Cup Illustrated*, and to Steve Waid, Tom Higgins, and Deb Williams at *NASCAR Winston Cup Scene*. Thanks also to Steve Ballard and Rudy Martzke at *USA Today* and to Stephen Madden and Dave Mingy at *Sports Illustrated*.

Don Hawk, Jr., president of Dale Earnhardt Incorporated, was instrumental in helping me understand the business opportunities for drivers. Thanks also to Ron Miller at Performance PR Plus and Bill Seaborn at Action Sports Management.

I owe a great deal to Jimmy Johnson, vice president and general manager at Hendrick Motorsports, who explained the advantages of a multiteam organization. Thanks also to Kathy Thompson, Fields Jackson, and Joe Washington at Washington Erving Motorsports.

Wall Street is waking up to the investment possibilities in NASCAR. Kevin Daly at Hoefer & Arnett, Breck Wheeler at J.C. Bradford, and Bo Cheadle at Montgomery Securities all shared investment opinions.

Rick Horrow at Horrow Sports Ventures, Mark Dyer, president of NASCAR Café, Barry Frank at IMG, and Shelley Morrison at Starwave Corporation added significant insight.

I am especially indebted to Mark Johnson, president of PRIMEDIA, who took the time to read the entire manuscript and offered many valuable ideas. Thank you, Mark.

John Wiley & Sons has done an outstanding job with this project. I wish to thank my publisher, Myles Thompson, for his continued support. A special thanks to Joan O'Neil, marketing director, and Andrea Abbott, marketing manager, who enthusiastically embraced the book; and to Jennifer Pincott, assistant editor, who is efficiency personified. Thanks also to Mary Daniello, the associate managing

ACKNOWLEDGMENTS

editor at Wiley, and to Nancy Marcus Land and Maryan Malone at Publications Development Company for their capable editorial work.

Laurie Harper, at Sebastian Literary Agency, is an outstanding agent. She has represented my interests admirably, thus allowing me the pleasure of working in peace. Thanks, Laurie.

For her professionalism, good judgment, and good humor, special thanks to my writing partner, Maggie Stuckey of Portland, Oregon. From day one, she added organizational logic, clarity, and pizazz to the writing of this book. In addition to being a talented writer and editor, she is something of a magician. From three thousand miles away, she can get inside my head and understand what I meant to say but didn't. Maggie Stuckey is one of the best in this business, and I am fortunate she is in my corner.

As you can see, book writing requires the efforts of many people. Even so, any mistakes or omissions are mine and mine alone.

Writing a book takes a great deal of time. For this project it also took a great deal of travel, which required me to be away from my family on several occasions. Some guys buy a convertible when they turn forty; I went racing. From the bottom of my heart, thanks to my family for their patience and forbearance. Truly, this book would have not been possible without their love and support. While I was busy writing and racing, my wife Maggie managed our household with grace and good cheer. She is a great mother and a wonderful wife. She is also my best friend.

R. G. H.

CONTENTS

The NASCAR Way

1

RIDING WITH ELMO

IT WASN'T UNTIL we came out of turn four at South Carolina's Darlington Raceway, that hot Sunday afternoon in September, that I really began to feel the full power of stock car racing. I had read about it, studied it, attended races, talked to drivers and team owners, and I thought I understood this quintessential American sport. But nothing prepares you for the *feeling* of tearing around a modern speedway at ninety miles an hour, the car holding a tight curve while tilting on a twenty-five-degree bank.

Fortunately, Elmo had a firm grip on the wheel of the slick black Pontiac Trans-Am, the official pace car of the Mountain Dew Southern 500. Safely belted into the passenger seat, all I had to do was grip my knees, open my eyes, and try to remember to breathe.

Elmo Langley, NASCAR's pace car official, sat stoically in the driver's seat. With a headset and attached microphone, he was in constant communication with the track tower as we headed down the front stretch. The radio crackled, "Second time by." Elmo flipped a switch and barked his response: "Ten-four, tower." He flexed the fingers of his hands, already perfectly positioned in the racer's "10 and

2" formation, and then suddenly picked up speed and punched the Trans-Am across the start–finish line.

The function of the pace car is to lead the race drivers in several controlled laps around the track as they gradually come up to speed. Elmo and I had two more laps to complete before the green flag would drop, signaling the start of the race. Directly behind us, neatly aligned in rows of two, thundered forty-two of the world's fastest stock cars.

Those drivers had earned their spot in this race two days before, in Friday's qualifying run, racing one lap against the clock. The driver with the fastest qualifying time gets the most desired position: the first row, on the inside; drivers call it "sitting on the pole." The second fastest qualifier gets the outside pole—the outside lane of the first row. The third and fourth qualifiers make up the second row, and so on down through the forty-second spot.

On the Friday before, Dale Jarrett took the pole for the Southern 500 by speeding around the track at 170.934 miles per hour. Jeff Gordon won the outside pole with a speed of 170.833. The slowest qualifier posted a speed of 166 miles an hour.

It's hard for most of us to conceive just how fast that is. I have driven calmly on the interstate at seventy miles an hour and even one time well over eighty. Just because my wife started to yell at me to slow down didn't mean I couldn't handle the car. But 170? That's twice as fast as I have ever been in a car. Today, during the pace laps, we're doing only ninety miles an hour, and yet it feels very different from my freeway escapade, particularly since just ahead of us is turn one, which angles straight up and then sharp left. My instincts are to ease up. Elmo has no intention of doing that. I try, unsuccessfully, to calm myself by calculating that we are going only half as fast as the cars behind us will, when the race begins.

Stock car drivers do things in cars that would make the rest of us faint. Try to imagine driving 100 miles an hour, then 120, then 160. Imagine keeping up that pace for three and a half hours; that's how long it will take to log 500 miles (that's what the 500 in "Southern 500" means). Now imagine forty-one other cars around you, all doing the same thing, just inches away from you, scraping against the side of your car and nudging your bumper as they try to pass you. And you can *never* slack off.

How fast are you willing to drive? How close are you willing to get to other cars? As you head into a turn, does your right foot tremble? Does your left foot come over and push down hard on your right foot to keep it from involuntarily lifting off the accelerator? To win a stock car race means that you are willing to drive faster than anybody else on the track. It means that you drive as fast as your nerves will let you go—and then faster. You, and every other driver in NASCAR, must forever chase the answer to the ultimate question: How fast is fast enough?

NASCAR's stock car racing is action-packed combat. There is no room for cowards in this sport. Once the green flag drops, the excitement, the danger, the intensity never stop.

As Elmo motored into turn one, the pace car began to drift high up on the banked turn. Elmo found his groove, where the car ran comfortably, only a few feet from the white concrete barrier that surrounded the track. The harder Elmo drove into the corner, the more I stiffened. Suddenly, halfway through turns one and two, the centrifugal force surged down on us. It felt like someone punched me right in the gut. My poker face blown, I gasped for air.

I sneaked a look at Elmo. His eyes were focused straight ahead, his hands held the wheel firmly, and although the microphone still covered his mouth, I could plainly see a smile. I rather think Elmo

Langley, a former stock car driver himself, enjoyed watching this self-confident writer from Philadelphia begin to squirm.

For the first time, I looked straight out the back window. Again I reached loudly for air. Dale Jarrett's Ford Quality Care Thunderbird and Jeff Gordon's DuPont Chevrolet were inches from our back bumper. Both drivers were weaving back and forth, heating their tires for more traction, their engines grunting and snorting like two thoroughbreds. Down the line, the entire pack of stock cars, two by two, were going through the same ritual. Those cars that weren't weaving back and forth were lunging forward in spurts as drivers punched and poked at their accelerators.

The pack had become anxious and unruly. I knew if Elmo slowed the slightest, that train of forty-two stock cars would run us down. But Elmo didn't slow. Instead, as we came out of turn two, he pushed the pace car far out ahead. One after another, the pack quickly fell in behind us as we began to run down the backstretch.

The 50,000 fans who lined the track were already on their feet yelling, waving, and cheering. Tyler Tower, a new state-of-the-art bleacher and concourse, stretched out a quarter of a mile ahead of us—twenty-five rows from ground level to the very top, twenty-five rows of pandemonium. To our left, the infield, the open area enclosed by the track, was crammed full of recreational vehicles, buses, and pickup trucks. Each was cleverly designed with a platform holding chairs, stereo systems, and sofas, and atop them all were about 25,000 more fans, fists raised in salute as the pack made its way down the track.

Today's event had become the most important race of the year because Dale Jarrett, sitting on the pole in the No. 88 car, was in a position to win $1 million if he crossed the finish line first. The Southern 500 is just one race in the series known as the Winston Cup, which consists of thirty-two separate races run between

February and November each year. NASCAR, the racing organization that dominates the sport, sanctions eleven other series, but the Winston Cup is the premier series, with the most prestige, the most attention, and the most prize money. Since 1985, the RJR Nabisco Company, which sponsors the Winston Cup series, has announced a $1 million bonus to any driver who could win three of the four major races in the series.

This year Dale Jarrett had a good shot at winning the bonus. He had already won the Daytona 500 and then the Coca-Cola 600 at Charlotte Motor Speedway. Now, the only things standing between him and a million bucks were forty-one other stock car drivers and "the meanest asphalt ever laid by man"—Darlington Raceway.

Darlington Raceway, NASCAR's oldest, is rich in history. Practically every driver who has ever raced at NASCAR's top level has had to run at Darlington, and not one among them doesn't believe it is the toughest track on the circuit.

Most racetracks are oval in shape, and so is Darlington, except that it is egg-shaped rather than a perfect oval. Turns one and two are tighter than three and four—a radius of 525 feet, compared to 600 feet. As you head into turn one, the car wants to slide up the racetrack and hit the wall. If you get through one and two without brushing the wall, you can punch it down the backstretch at nearly 190 miles an hour. Then, when you get to turns three and four, which are wider, you can keep your speed at 150 or 155 if you take to the high line. The problem comes when you come out of turn four. Just as you head for the straightaway, the centrifugal force caused by the high speed pushes the car outward. There is not a driver who hasn't brushed the wall in turn four, and many have smacked it dead-on.

Doyle Ford, a NASCAR official who flagged races at Darlington for years, once asked Richard Petty why the drivers run so close to the wall at turn four. "He gave me that big ol' grin," Ford remembered, "and said it was because the closer you are to the wall the less it hurts when you hit it."[1]

Because Darlington is such a difficult layout, drivers have learned they have to race not only other drivers but the track itself. Winning here takes a delicate balance between aggressiveness toward the other drivers, and patience with the track. If you run too smooth, the other drivers will pass you; if you run too hard, you'll become another black stripe along the white concrete barriers. This give-and-take is difficult to maintain for 500 miles, and that is what has earned Darlington the reputation as The Track Too Tough to Tame.

The stock cars that stretched out in a long line behind Elmo and me were a solid Detroit mixture, including Chevrolet Monte Carlo, Ford Thunderbird, and Pontiac Grand Prix. That's what the term "stock car" means—a regular car off the production line. In the early days of stock car racing, the cars were exactly that. Today, the term is more symbolic than literal. In silhouette, the cars tearing around the track do indeed look like ordinary Chevies or Fords. In fact, a template of a stock race car will fit amazingly well when placed over its cousin at the automobile dealership lot. But this is where the similarities end.

Although each stock car is equipped with a rather ordinary standard 358-cubic-inch V8 motor, specialized engine builders have learned how to turn them into 700-horsepower monsters. In addition, a chassis specialist, by manipulating the front and rear suspension, shocks, and tires, can mold a stock car to a racetrack. When completed, the ultimate stock car creation is literally a rocket ship on wheels, able to blast around a track at 200 mph.

To fully appreciate stock car racing, you have to understand not one passion but two. As Elmo and I led the forty-two cars around the track, the yelling and cheering that followed us were not only for the drivers, but for the cars they drove.

Spread out across Darlington Raceway was a battalion of fans who worshipped Chevrolets and an equally impressive battalion who favored Fords. In the back row, you could even make out a smaller platoon of fans who cheered for Pontiacs. Occasionally, stock car fans may shift their allegiance from one driver to another, but it is rare that a Ford fan switches to Chevrolet and they say not until hell freezes over will a Chevrolet fan ever support Ford.

For stock car fans, race day begins at dawn. Even though the checkered flag that starts the race will not be waved until 1:00 P.M., it can take all morning to get to the track. Most racetracks were built miles from the center of town, where land was both cheap and plentiful. The plan for the day must include not only the calculation for distance driven but for the time it takes to park once you have reached "the biggest traffic jam in the history of the world."

Over the years, racetrack officials and state and local police have worked hard at improving traffic flow before and after a stock car race. Even so, with upward of 50,000 fans rapidly descending on Darlington Raceway, bottlenecks are inevitable.

Whereas most traffic jams are a bore, stock car fans have found interesting ways to pass the time while miles of cars crawl toward parking lots. The first order of business is to raise the colors. On almost every car heading to a race, prominently displayed on a back or side window is a sign showing a driver's name, his car, or simply his number. Sometimes flags with the same inscriptions hang from poles attached to the side of a car. As cars with competitors' flags pull alongside each other in the traffic, fans from both cars roll down their windows and launch into a fierce but friendly debate on the qualities of their driver versus the field. The closer you get to the track, the more vocal the fans become.

Finally parked and unloaded, fans by the thousands parade toward the racetrack. Attending a stock car race is very much like attending a state fair. Once inside the perimeter gates, the atmosphere is clearly festive. Even though the race is not set to begin for a few more hours, there is plenty to do, see, and purchase.

Lining both sides of the walkways surrounding the track are fifty to sixty trailers, giving the racetrack the look of a carnival midway. Almost every driver has a trailer (some have two) outfitted with T-shirts, sweatshirts, golf shirts, baseball caps, mugs, water bottles, coolers, license plates, flags, stickers, pins, towels, floats, Frisbees, and blankets—all emblazoned with the driver's likeness. The trailer itself is brightly painted in the colors of the driver's car, with his name and number splashed across its side. With sides open, the trailer reveals an entire store of driver memorabilia.

If you are attending a stock car race for the first time, you'd be smart to stop by a trailer and adopt a stock car driver for the race. This simple act of allegiance will save you from having to answer, for the next three hours, the same question over and over: "Who's your favorite driver?"

If you are unable to make up your mind which driver you want to support, you could always devote yourself to an automobile manufacturer. Both Ford and Chevrolet have trailers here, with as many licensed products as the drivers have. If you look hard enough, you can even pick up some Pontiac mementos, probably at the trailer of a driver who races in a Pontiac Grand Prix.

If you need time to decide which driver to root for, you can stop by a food trailer where the lines are forming for hot dogs, hamburgers, french fries, cotton candy, funnel cakes, coffee, and sodas. There is plenty of cold beer too, but to purchase it you have to wait until you get inside the track.

Where the trailers end, the hospitality village begins. Corporations are quickly learning the benefit of entertaining their clients at stock car races. Sonoco, a large South Carolina paper product manufacturer that once brought as few as ten guests to the Southern 500, purchased tent space for 400 for the 1996 season. Each year, corporations vie for the limited number of hospitality tents that become available.

According to many regulars, there is no more beautiful place to entertain clients and guests than Darlington Raceway. The hospitality village itself is outlined in white picket fences that surround beautifully appointed white and yellow striped tents. Flower boxes hang at each entrance.

Inside the tents are dozens of tables covered with white linen cloths, each attended by waiters anxious to deliver any requested food or beverage. Closed-circuit televisions are positioned throughout, broadcasting the latest news about the upcoming race. Show cars, exact replicas of the race cars, are sprinkled around the village. Guests are given periodic tours of the garage and pit areas, where they can watch the crews prepare the stock cars for the race. When they return to their tents, they find a celebrated stock car driver waiting to sign autographs or to chat with them about racing.

If your company was not lucky enough to get one of the available hospitality tents, perhaps you can manage to get invited to visit one of the corporate suites. High above the track, you can watch the action in air-conditioned comfort while enjoying a catered dinner served on linen-covered tables. Darlington Raceway leases four corporate suites, for $100,000 each per year, to PepsiCo, RJR Nabisco, Unocal Oil, and Anheuser-Busch.

Most of the arriving fans ultimately head for the grandstands. As they enter through the gates, they are treated to professionally land-scaped grounds and manicured flower beds. Freshly planted mums are surrounded with ample mulch; the grass is neatly trimmed and edged. Crepe myrtles heavy with lush purple blossoms surround the track, interrupted occasionally by palmetto palms, the official tree of South Carolina. There is no litter. Groundskeepers constantly patrol the track on the chance that some fans have missed the lined garbage cans stationed every fifty feet. There are ample bathrooms, and they are spotless, with attendants standing nearby to assist as needed.

Over the years, the makeup of race fans has changed. If you attend your first race with preconceived ideas about the fans, be prepared for a surprise. Overall, nearly 30 percent of stock car fans have an annual income over $50,000; 38 percent are female. One testament to the changing demographics: Texas Motor Speedway, the ultramodern superspeedway outside Dallas–Fort Worth that opened for business in 1997, has twice as many women's bathrooms as men's. Today, at Darlington, almost half the fans are women, most of them walking hand in hand with their husbands, and many have brought their children.

In the beginning, stock car racing was a sport for the rowdiest and roughest. But no more. Today's stock car races are family events. Uniformed security officers are on constant patrol throughout the track, to defuse inappropriate behavior and maintain a family atmosphere. This is a deliberate, proactive strategy by the track owners. Savvy owners quickly learned that a well-kept, clean, and orderly grandstand not only enticed race fans back each year, but also allowed the track to aggressively price its seats—and it has worked. The approximately 50,000 grandstand seats at the Darlington 500—one of the smallest NASCAR tracks—have an average ticket price of $60 each.

The infield, the open area inside the track itself, has become the last bastion for stock car racing's most passionate fans. They travel hundreds of miles in their recreational vehicles, campers, pickup trucks, and vans, and they are equipped to make the infield their home for three days. They are determined not to miss one minute of racing: the qualifying runs and the practices on Friday, the support race and then more practicing on Saturday, and the featured race on Sunday, with all its festivities.

In the 1950s and 1960s, the infield at a racetrack was very much like the Wild West. The local sheriff would set up a temporary jail in the infield; it was far easier to lock up offenders there than to drag them out across the track. Music blared all night long while motorcycles roared up and down the lanes. But today, this behavior is as outdated as dirt tracks, dirty bathrooms, and wooden benches.

In recent years, track owners have, as with the rest of their facilities, substantially upgraded the infields. At Darlington Raceway, president Jim Hunter has promoted several programs designed specifically to improve the quality of the infield: the 4th Turn Club, the President's Suite, and Azalea Terrace.

The 4th Turn Club is a large corporate hospitality tent placed in the infield at turn four. Here, a corporation can invite as many as 100 guests to watch the race up close. At the end of the front-stretch, just before turn one, stands the President's Suite, where the track owner entertains special guests in a clubhouse setting or out on a wooden deck overlooking the track. The Azalea Terrace, located on turns one and two, was designed for families. Each individual camping space is outlined with white linked chains hung between ornate posts, and each space has its own entrance decorated with painted barrels full of azaleas.

The marketing strategy now being played out in the infield has produced the desired results: higher-quality facilities commanding higher prices. Fans can park their recreational vehicle in a reserved infield spot for $175 for the weekend, plus $75 per person. To enjoy a three-day package in the Azalea Terrace, including a private space and four infield tickets, the price tag is $500.

On Thursday afternoon, the infield at Darlington was nothing but a large empty field surrounded by a dead-quiet track. By Friday night, a small city had taken shape. Out came the tents, barbecues, and lawn furniture. Kids rode the vast complex on bicycles while the adults analyzed and debated Friday's qualifying results. Stereos blasted out country music and southern rock. Old friends caught up with each other and new friends were made. Horseshoes is the official sport, burgers and beer are the official cuisine, and racing is the language.

As Elmo and I safely exited the fourth turn and headed down the frontstretch, it was easy to spot the men in white and red NASCAR uniforms. In all, sixty officials were on hand, strategically placed around the track. At the start–finish line, two officials stood high in the flag stand, and one was positioned directly across the track, where video equipment was taping the entire race. Two officials stood at the entrance to pit row, and two more were posted at its exit. There were spotters at each turn, and several officials patrolled the garage area.

During the race, over half of NASCAR's officials are positioned along pit row, where their job is to examine closely the actions of the crews and the safety of the cars. There are rules that dictate how many crew members can come over the pit wall to work on a car, and rules that dictate when a car is safe to be on the track. Any violation of NASCAR's rules can result in penalties ranging from a fifteen-second delay before returning to the race, to being placed down several laps against the field. In some cases,

NASCAR can "black-flag" a car, meaning the car must leave the track for repairs.

NASCAR rules are designed to promote close, competitive racing, which the fans want, in a way that maintains parity and does not unduly favor the well-financed teams. The paramount force behind all the rules, however, is the safety of both the drivers and the fans. Everyone in NASCAR is aware of the potential for injury with so many machines running in close quarters at such high speeds, and so the rules and regulations are vigorously enforced.

A NASCAR-sanctioned motorsports event, like the Southern 500, is officiated by NASCAR and conducted in accordance with its rules. These rules cover not only the race, but all periods leading up to and following it, including registration, inspections, time trials, qualifying races, practices, and postrace inspections.

In exchange for having NASCAR officials conduct the race, and for the opportunity to promote a NASCAR event, the track owner pays NASCAR a fee. In addition, NASCAR has been able to increase its revenues by licensing its name and by awarding official corporate sponsorships. Today, there are NASCAR restaurants, retail stores, and entertainment parks. More than twenty-five corporations pay NASCAR for the privilege of becoming an official sponsor to the sport.

Corporate sponsorship is the backbone to this sport. As Elmo motors down the frontstretch, a glance to the left gives me a quick visual summary of corporate America's appetite for stock car racing. There, standing before the grandstand at full attention, are the pit crews. Once the race is underway, their job is the most critical of all, next to the drivers themselves. When the race car pulls in for a pit stop, every fraction of a second counts. Working in well-rehearsed choreography, the pit crew will change all four tires and refuel the car in twenty seconds. For now, however, standing still, they represent human billboards.

Each crew member's uniform is brightly decorated with the logo of the team's corporate sponsor. In the earliest years, a pit crew uniform consisted of blue jeans and T-shirts. But today, with the influx of corporate sponsors, the pit crew uniform has become valuable advertising space. The driver, too, when he appears, will be wearing a uniform totally covered with insignia from all his team's sponsors. The pit wagon, a toolbox on wheels, is also decorated in the colors and emblem of the team's corporate sponsor.

Stock car racing is no longer dominated by tobacco, beer, and automotive products. Today, there are over 250 corporate sponsors associated with stock car racing, including seventy Fortune 500 companies with highly sophisticated marketing plans. Attesting to their awareness of the "new" stock car fan base, sponsors include companies whose products are traditionally bought by women: Kellogg's cereals, Tide, Gatorade, Pepsi, Coca-Cola, and Kodak film as well as The Family Channel, The Cartoon Network, QVC Network, and Circuit City. Because race teams, racetracks, and NASCAR itself depend heavily on corporate sponsorship, the sport has made participation both affordable and flexible.

Corporations with large sponsorship budgets can choose to sponsor an entire race. The Southern 500 is sponsored by Mountain Dew, a division of PepsiCo, which in turn supplies the soft drinks for the race. Although the race has been customarily referred to as the Southern 500, its official name is the Mountain Dew Southern 500. Companies with more modest budgets can make a presence by running an ad in the souvenir program. Its 132 color pages are filled with ads for Canon cameras, Lowe's Home Improvement, McDonald's, MasterCard, Kmart, Craftsman tools, True Value Hardware, Gatorade, Burger King, and Nations Bank.

Special awards, within each race, allow corporations to advertise their support of stock car racing. For example, Anheuser-Busch sponsors the Pole Award; the team that wins the pole for the race receives a cash bonus. There are awards for the best mechanic, the best pit strategy, and the driver who leads the most miles during the race, and there are many others.

In addition to sponsoring a race, advertising at a race, sponsoring various awards programs, and becoming an official sponsor of NASCAR, corporations can take the ultimate role in motorsports advertising by sponsoring a team. NASCAR does not allow any advertising on the car roof or doors, where the car's number appears, but every other surface on the car is a blank canvas, and corporations squeeze every inch they can: on the hood, trunk lid, edge of the trunk, and rear quarter panels, and above the back bumper. Teams sell these spaces either individually or in packages, at a cost ranging from $250,000 to several million dollars. Companies with smaller budgets can also buy advertising space using twenty-six-inch decals, for as little as $62,000 per season.

Few corporations are willing to spend millions of advertising dollars in hopes that consumers will eventually find their logos or messages. For that amount of investment, corporations will single out captured audiences where the gross number of potential consumers justifies the marketing investment. NASCAR racing works. The growing attendance at racetracks, coupled with the demonstrated brand loyalty fans feel toward companies that sponsor their favorite driver, has helped race teams solicit greater corporate sponsorship. But it is clear that the leverage stock car racing has in selling itself to advertisers is increasingly based on its television and radio audience.

More than any other single factor, television is credited for stock car racing's phenomenal growth. Because television, both cable and

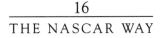

network, still reaches the widest audience, it is the preferred vehicle for corporate advertising.

Although network television first broadcast live stock car races—with CBS's coverage of the infamous 1979 Daytona 500—it was cable television that significantly increased the television audience for racing. Today, cable television has become the authority on stock car racing, as evidenced by ESPN's fourteen Emmy awards for covering the sport.

For the Southern 500, ESPN's cameras were everywhere. Several cameras were stationed high above the control tower on the frontstretch; in the control booth just below, three broadcasters called the entire race. Other cameras were stationed above the corporate suites in turn one, down the backstretch, and at turn four. So as not to miss any of the coverage, crews with portable cameras were roaming up and down pit row, collecting periodic updates and inside opinions from the teams' crew chiefs. This is the only sport where the coach is interviewed while the game is still on.

Today, all Winston Cup races are televised nationally on five networks: CBS, ABC, ESPN, TBS, and TNN. The networks are also scrambling to air two other NASCAR race series: the Busch Grand National, rated just below the Winston Cup, and the Craftsman Truck series, an increasingly popular series featuring pickup trucks. The rush to line up more NASCAR races is easily explained, particularly for cable: viewership ratings. On ESPN, only NFL football outdraws NASCAR Winston Cup racing. Generally, the ratings for stock car races surpass nonplayoff basketball, baseball, and hockey.

As Elmo cruised down the frontstretch for the last time before the green flag, Doyle Ford, NASCAR's official starter, held out one finger to the pack. Elmo reached down and switched off the yellow caution lights. That signal, everyone knew, meant the next time by, the race would begin.

Around turns one and two and down the backstretch, Elmo kept the same speed. But as I looked out the back window for the last time, I noticed that the pack began to tighten. There was no more weaving and bobbing, no more punching and poking. Like close-order drill, all forty-two stock cars were cruising at attention. With less than a lap to go, each driver was focused on the start.

I had not felt the vibration the first two times around the track, but now it was impossible to ignore. The deep rumble of Detroit firepower was actually reverberating through the pace car. The incredible force of forty-two stock car engines tightly bundled was creating intense sound waves that were bouncing off the track into the car and through the seat.

A stock car has swagger. A Detroit 700-horsepower engine makes a sound like no other. The sound is not Japanese, not German, and certainly not Swedish. It is uniquely American, a deep rumbling sound, unrefined but incredibly powerful. It is a sound from the 1950s, when hot rods cruised, after dark, up and down the main streets of our small towns. It is a sound that announced the comings and goings of a new generation of young Americans who, set free from the burdens of World War II, were now full of promise and opportunity.

But there is another sound at the racetrack, and it is every bit as powerful as the stock cars beating down the backstretch at Darlington. If you talk to enough people, observe, and listen carefully, you will hear it clearly. It is the hardworking sound of a business, the throb of pure uninhibited capitalism that guarantees to pay only for performance.

The sounds of a successful business are as exciting to me as the roar of stock cars heading toward the green flag. What makes the business of stock car racing so exciting is the behind-the-scenes shuffling, the unstoppable forward progress that is now taking place. It is the sound of bulldozers carving out new racetracks, and construction cranes adding new seats. It is the sound of corporations altering their marketing strategy, and advertising agencies plotting new campaigns. It is the sound of broadcast and cable networks competing aggressively for the rights to televise races. It is the sound of sports fans switching the channels on their sets; and when the television and radio have been turned off, it is the sound of clicking laptop computers connecting to Internet sites and chat rooms.

Most of all, it is the sound of a special time in sports that many have long since forgotten. To the surprise of many sportswriters, the sound they hear in stock car racing today is the same sound they heard in baseball in the 1920s and 1930s, in football in the 1960s, and in basketball in the 1970s. It is the sound of humility and gratitude and enthusiasm. It is the sound of athletes who tell you—and who mean it—that they are no bigger than the fans who come out and support them. It is the sound of autographs being signed, of smiling pictures being snapped, and of kids collecting heroes. It is what is best about American sports, and that sound you hear is the shift that is occurring as stock car racing surges ahead.

With seconds to go before the start of the race, Elmo was no longer grinning. His face was a study of concentration. There would be no mistakes. The vibrating rumble that filled the pace car began to swell. Every person in the crowd was standing, cheering. I could see the yelling but no sounds rose above the thunder that was building behind us, filling the bowl of the track.

Elmo glanced in the rearview mirror one last time, then banked hard left to duck down into the pits. The tires squealed as he crammed down on the brakes. Before we could stop, the pack had already jumped to life. In perfect tight formation, they passed us by, picking up speed faster and faster. The green flag was out. All forty-two stock cars punched the accelerator at the same time, and the ground shook.

2

RULES OF THE ROAD

STOCK CAR RACING was born in the South, the boisterous legacy of the daredevil moonshine drivers who tore up and down the back roads of Appalachia during the 1930s and 1940s.

For years, hardscrabble farmers in the mountains had been making their own whiskey, just as they made their own tools, clothes, and furniture. But it wasn't until Prohibition in 1919 that mountaineers discovered that the sippin' whiskey they made for themselves was worth cash money to the folks in town. For many mountain families, bootlegging was their only source of income in the winter months.

Surprisingly, the 21st Amendment, which repealed Prohibition in 1933, did not reduce the demand for moonshine. By then, the devastating effects of the Great Depression had spread throughout the nation. The whiskey-drinking city folks needed to save every penny, and the mountain families depended on the income from moonshine more than ever. At the same time, the federal government needed the revenue from tax on alcohol to fund the many New Deal programs established to counteract the Depression.

By the 1940s, the government began sending federal revenue agents into the Appalachian Mountains to stop illegal whiskey manufacturing. To avoid the revenuers, the mountaineers hid their stills and began to work only at night—hence the term "moonshiner." Drivers would begin their delivery runs after midnight and be safely home before daybreak. The whole business of making, loading, and delivering moonshine occurred under the cover of darkness.

In a stepped-up game of cat and mouse, the revenuers searched for stills by day and staked out the roads at night. To stay ahead, moonshine drivers constantly tinkered with their cars, trying to eke out a few extra horsepower and to improve the suspension so the car would handle better. It wasn't easy barreling over hills and valleys in the middle of the night, dirt kicking up everywhere, and your car loaded down with twenty-five cases of white lightning. To keep out of jail, the car had to be perfect.

After a while, the hot rods that hauled moonshine in the middle of the night became famous. Each moonshine car got a nickname—the Black Ghost, the Grey Ghost, the Midnight Traveler, Old Faithful.[1] At the breakfast table, over at the diner, out in the fields, everyone was swapping stories about their favorite cars and drivers.

What happened next was all but inevitable.

The history books tell us that the first stock car race among moonshiners occurred in the mid-1930s "in a cow pasture in the town of Stockbridge, Georgia."[2] It seems that a few moonshiners started arguing about who had the fastest car and who was the better driver. To settle the dispute, someone carved out a quarter-mile dirt track in the middle of a farmer's field. Each sport has a beginning. For stock car racing, that beginning was a farm field in the South.

The first race, unannounced, drew about fifty people. The next time, over 100 people showed up to watch the moonshiners slamming and banging into each other. When thousands began lining up to get a chance to watch a race, the farmer fenced off the pasture, put up a gate, and charged admission. The drivers' payout continued to climb, too, and eventually the cash prize at the checkered flag was worth as much as running moonshine from Wilkes County to Charlotte. It didn't take long before moonshine drivers began to show up on a regular basis.

If you were a good moonshine runner, there was a pretty good chance you had the skills to become a great stock car driver. First of all, you had to be able to drive well on dirt. In the earliest days, all stock car races were held at dirt tracks. On the weekends, stock car drivers would travel to state fairgrounds, horse racetracks, or even plowed-up fields. After driving over 100 miles an hour on the dirt roads of North Carolina in the middle of the night while being chased by revenuers, the moonshiners looked at these smooth, level, quarter-mile racetracks, crossed their arms, rocked back on their heels, and grinned.

The Flock brothers—Tim, Bob, and Fonty—drove for their uncle, Peachtree Williams, who had one of the biggest stills in Georgia. Buddy Shuman also ran whiskey and drove stock cars. But the most famous bootlegger ever to drive stock cars was Junior Johnson. Junior ran whiskey for his daddy, Glenn Johnson, who had the biggest and most profitable moonshine operation in Wilkes County, North Carolina.

All the things Junior learned about driving a moonshine car on dirt made him almost unstoppable at the racetrack. Other drivers would slow their cars going into turns and then punch them again on the straightaway. But not Junior. He knew how to accelerate through the turns simply by cocking the wheel hard to the left and fishtailing the rear end of the car, all without slowing down. Junior had perfected the power slide. He had done it night after night in the hills of North Carolina, and it didn't occur to him you couldn't do it at the racetrack.

Stock car racing takes guts. If you ran moonshine, courage was never the question. Junior Johnson loved dirt racing because it gave him a chance to mix it up with the other drivers. He loved banging on other cars, slamming into their sides, and bouncing off the guardrail. It has been said that driving superspeedways, like Daytona, for 500 miles tests the car, but driving dirt tests the man.

At about the same time as the Georgia farmer was setting up his field for racing, an auto mechanic and part-time race driver in the Washington, DC, area made a personal decision that would profoundly and permanently change the course of stock car racing.

Big Bill France

Modern-day stock car racing owes its success—some would say, its very existence—to one man: William Henry Getty France, known even now, years after his death, as "Big Bill."

Bill France was racing cars at dirt tracks in the Maryland suburbs of Washington, DC, by the time he was twenty. He was a pretty good driver and, like most others in the sport, a decent mechanic. When he wasn't racing, he was usually working on cars in garages and service stations. At that same time, Anne Bledsoe, known to all as "Annie B," was attending nursing school at Children's Hospital in Washington. One night, at a local dance, a mutual friend introduced Bill to Annie B. They were a perfect match and, in 1931, Bill and Annie B married. Three years later, tired of the cold winters, Bill packed up Annie B and their infant son, Bill Jr., and headed for Florida.

It was France's intention to settle in Miami, but after a quick tourist stopover in Daytona Beach, he decided there was no need to go any farther. He rented an apartment for the family and soon found work, first as a painter and then later as an auto mechanic. Before long, France opened his own gas station on Daytona's main street. Big Bill made friends quickly; in no time, his gas station became the favorite hangout for the race drivers and mechanics who gravitated to Daytona.

Daytona Beach, with its hard-packed sandy beaches 500 yards wide and 25 miles long, was already known among automobile racers as the Speed Capital of the world. It was here that the famous English racer Sir Malcolm Campbell came each year to try to set new land speed records. By the time the young France family arrived, Speedweek at Daytona Beach had become a motorsports tradition and an important source of revenue for local businesses.

France stood on the beach in 1935, along with thousands of others, to watch Sir Malcolm attempt to break the 300 mph barrier. It never happened. Strong headwinds off the Atlantic held the top speeds to 275 and created dangerous driving conditions. It seemed that land speed records, at Daytona Beach, had reached their limit. The following year, the cars and their drivers headed for the Bonneville Salt Flats of Utah.

The city fathers of Daytona Beach panicked. To keep the thousands of visitors—and their dollars—returning, business and community leaders struggled to continue Speedweek. They managed to put together races in 1936 and 1937, but both were poorly managed events and financial disasters. In early 1938, a delegation from the Daytona Beach Chamber of Commerce stopped by Bill France's gas station. After two failures, there was not going to be a race for 1938, unless they could convince Bill France to organize one.

Recruiting France was an inspired idea. His reputation was rising among the townspeople, and he was well liked by most area mechanics and race car drivers. He was a natural promoter, and from his own years as a racer he knew what worked in staging a race and what didn't. He had just one small problem: money.

In earlier Daytona races, France had driven a car owned by a local restaurateur named Charlie Reese. When France told Charlie about the beach race, Charlie agreed to foot the bill if France would do all the legwork; they would split the profits. In short order, the 1938 Beach Race was scheduled for July 4.

Word quickly spread that France was organizing the beach race; before long, three dozen racers were ready to go. When France wasn't signing up drivers, he was busy gathering prizes: a bottle of rum for each lap leader, a $2.50 credit at a local clothing store, two cases of Blue Ribbon Beer, a box of Hav-a-Tampa cigars, a case of Pennzoil motor oil, and a $25 credit toward purchasing a car at Dick Rose's used-car lot. The idea of sponsorships was beginning to take hold.

On the morning of July 4, the beach was filled with 4,500 spectators who had paid 50 cents to watch the race. The 1938 Daytona Beach Race was a great success. There were no controversies, the winners were dutifully paid, and city officials were delighted. That night, after all the bills were paid, France and Charlie split $200 in profit. Before sunrise, France was already planning the next beach race for Labor Day.

His enthusiasm for promoting Daytona's beach race was quickly evident. More grandstands and seats were added. A scoreboard was placed at the north turn, and loudspeakers were installed to keep fans informed about the leaders during the race.

France proposed a simple set of rules for each car, to ensure both a competitive race and the drivers' safety. The doors and hoods of each car had to be bolted down, and just in case anyone thought about cheating, there would be a postrace inspection of the winning cars before the prize money was paid. When France wasn't working on the track or on race regulations, he was gathering more sponsorships. By 1939, tickets for the Daytona Beach race were $1; with attendance sharply up, France's profits were in the thousands. The neophyte race promoter was now officially on his way.

The obligations of all men and women during World War II interrupted stock car racing. France's mechanical skills were sent to the shipyards to build submarine chasers, but his mind was constantly working on plans to improve the business of racing. When the war ended, France returned to Daytona Beach eager to start where he had left off. However, both the beach course and the grandstands were in sorry shape from the years of neglect. To start again required more capital than France had. Sadly, his good friend and financial partner Charlie Reese had passed away. Without Charlie's financial backing, France needed a different strategy.

He learned about an oval dirt track in Charlotte, North Carolina, that was available for rent, and decided to sponsor a 100-mile National Championship race there. He ran into his first snag when he invited local reporters to cover the upcoming event: they were reluctant to write about a "national championship" race when there was no official sanctioning body and no official set of rules. Remembering that the Automobile Association of America (AAA) had once sanctioned a Daytona Beach race, France contacted the organization. But AAA had no interest in sponsoring France's race; besides, they said, the whole concept of American stock cars racing each other was a dying fad.

What France did next was an important measure of the man. If AAA wasn't interested, he would organize his own sanctioning body. And he did. The National Championship Stock Car Circuit (NCSCC) would sponsor races every month at various sites, with a cumulative point system and winners' fund. So committed was France to this idea that he sent for Annie B to handle the NCSCC's books and arranged for someone to run the service station at Daytona Beach. Soon France was scheduling monthly races at tracks scattered throughout the Southeast.

1947 was the first full year of racing sanctioned by the National Championship Stock Car Circuit and, by everyone's estimate, it was a great success. Fonty Flock, the Georgia bootlegger, was crowned National Champion. The points fund, at the end of the year, was worth $3,000, and it was divided among the year's top finishers.

Still, France was troubled. Throughout the year, he had to deal with different rules at different tracks. Some track owners falsely advertised big purses that were never paid to the winners; some even took off with the gate receipts before the race concluded. Stock car racing had a reputation of being disorganized at best, crooked at worst. If the sport was ever to succeed, France knew it would require a central racing organization whose authority outranked all drivers, car owners, and track owners.

So Bill France took his next bold step. He invited racing's most influential members to a year-end meeting in Daytona Beach, to discuss the future of stock car racing. On the afternoon of December 14, 1947, atop the Streamline Hotel in downtown Daytona, Big Bill France stood up to address thirty-five of his colleagues.

He began by describing his vision: a central body whose sole purpose would be "to unite all stock car racing under one set of rules; to set up a benevolent fund and a national point standings whereby only one stock car driver would be crowned National Champion."[3] The rules, he declared, would have to be consistent, enforceable, and ironclad. Cheating would not be allowed. The regulations would be designed to ensure close competition, for they all knew that close side-by-side racing was what the fans cheered for. Finally, he argued, the organizing body should promote a racing division dedicated solely to standard street stock cars, the same cars that could be bought at automobile dealerships. Fans would love these races, France argued, because they could identify with the cars.

France sat down. After some debate, the group voted to form a national organization for stock car racing. To no one's surprise, Bill France was elected president of this yet unnamed body. A board of governors was also elected, with authority to develop bylaws and the rules of competition. The group also decided to incorporate the organization, and everyone at the meeting was invited to invest. Only four people did: Louis Ossinsky, a local attorney who exchanged legal services for shares of stock; Bill Tuthill and Ed Otto, both of them respected race promoters; and Bill France. The National Association for Stock Car Auto Racing (NASCAR) was officially incorporated on February 15, 1948.

The Early Years

The first order of business for NASCAR's board of governors was to appoint a technical committee that would formulate the rules and regulations for the sanctioning body. The technical committee set standards for engine size, safety, and fair competition. Only American-made cars would be allowed to compete.

Next, NASCAR took a hard look at safety, both for the driver and for the fans seated at the tracks. Drivers were required to be strapped into cars and they had to wear driving helmets.

Tracks were required to surround the racetrack with safety fences to prevent wheels and other parts of a car from accidentally flying into the stands.

In what was considered a revolutionary stance in those days, NASCAR guaranteed the purses for each race it sanctioned—no exceptions. Generally, the track owner was required to deposit the prize money with NASCAR before the race could start. Only a few times did NASCAR actually have to pay out of its own pocket the monies promised the race drivers. However financially painful, this act was instrumental in gaining the respect of the race drivers.

Lastly, NASCAR devised a national point system. No matter where they raced, as long as it was a NASCAR-sanctioned racetrack, the finishing drivers accumulated points that reflected their performance: so many points for first place, then second place, and so on. Track owners were required to place 7.5 percent of the prize money into a national points fund. At the end of the year, the leading drivers split the accumulated fund.

In its first year, the NASCAR organization sanctioned three different racing divisions: Strictly Stock, Modified Stock, and Roadsters. The Strictly Stock division would include full-size American cars with standard hoods, fenders, bumpers, and grilles—the very same parts as were listed in the manufacturers' parts catalogs. France instinctively knew there would be significant fan interest for this type of racing. What he couldn't overcome was the lack of available cars. After World War II, Detroit was slow in revamping production for passenger cars. The waiting list for many automobiles stretched for months.

So the 1948 racing season began with the modifieds and the roadsters. There were plenty of cars available for these two divisions. In the modified division, for instance, cars had to be 1937 or later models; they had to have windshields and fenders, but after that, almost any modification was allowed.

The Strictly Stock Division held its first race on a three-quarter-mile dirt track in Charlotte, North Carolina, on June 19, 1949, before 13,000 fans. The race was not without controversy. First across the finish line was Glenn Dunnaway. However, when it was discovered in a postrace inspection that Dunnaway's 1947 Ford had a wedge placed in the rear suspension (an old bootlegger trick to stiffen the springs and improve handling), he was promptly disqualified and first place was awarded to the second finisher, Jim Roper. The owner of Dunnaway's car sued NASCAR for the $2,000 prize money but lost. The judge ruled that NASCAR had the right to makes its own rules and therefore had the right to enforce them. It was an important day for NASCAR.

NASCAR went on to sanction eight Strictly Stock races in 1949. Red Byron, a driving legend from Atlanta, won the first championship. Lee Petty came in second, and the legendary bootlegging Flock brothers (Bob, Fonty, and Tim) finished third, fifth, and eighth respectively. At year end, France changed the name of the Strictly Stock Division to the Grand National Division. By borrowing the name of England's premier thoroughbred racing event, Bill France served notice to all that the Strictly Stocks were now NASCAR's headline division.

Twelve NASCAR Divisions

Today, NASCAR sanctions approximately 2,000 events each year in twelve separate divisions at more than 100 racetracks across the country. The organization has more than 52,000 members, including some of the best drivers, mechanics, and car owners in the world. In 1996, some 15,430,000 people attended NASCAR events, and 130,000,000 more watched on TV.[4]

Here are capsule descriptions of the twelve NASCAR racing divisions.

1. *Winston Cup.* This is NASCAR's premier racing series. Winston Cup racing is considered the most competitive form of motorsports in the world today; this is where you will find the most celebrated drivers.

When the RJR Reynolds Tobacco company, makers of Winston cigarettes, agreed to sponsor the Grand National series, the name was changed to Winston Cup. Today, Winston Cup racing is greatly supported by Chevrolet, Ford, and Pontiac, and the three primary cars are Chevrolet Monte Carlo, Ford Thunderbird, and Pontiac Grand Prix. Rules permit the use of the Buick Regal, Mercury Cougar, and Oldsmobile Cutlass; but without factory support, no owner considers racing these models. Only the most recent three years' models are allowed.

2. *Busch Series, Grand National Division.* Second only to Winston Cup racing in fan attendance and prize money. Typically, this series is the training ground for future Winston Cup drivers. Busch Grand National cars are very similar to Winston Cup cars, except that they run with less horsepower and are 100 pounds lighter and five inches shorter.

3. *Craftsman Truck Series.* NASCAR's newest racing series. Pickup trucks are the best-selling vehicles in the United States, and race fans relate to them with great enthusiasm. The racing is competitive and intense. Each pickup truck is built to specifications that are very similar to those of Winston Cup cars.

4. *Winston Racing Series.* NASCAR sanctions weekly races at over 100 short tracks across the country. The series is divided into ten regions. A point system ties all of the regions together. At the end of the year, each region produces a champion and, based on total points, a National Champion is crowned. The Winston Racing series is a grass-roots level of racing and is very popular among fans at smaller local tracks.

5. *Winston West Series.* One of NASCAR's oldest racing divisions; tracks are located in Arizona, California, Colorado, Nevada, Oregon, and Washington. Cars are very similar to Winston Cup cars—in fact, Winston West drivers compete against Winston Cup drivers twice a year.

6. *Busch North Series.* Races are held in Connecticut, Maine, Massachusetts, New Hampshire, New York, and Pennsylvania. Considered one of the fastest-growing racing series, Busch North races are often held in combination with Busch Grand National races, for both series feature similar cars.

7. *Busch All-Star Tour.* This is the only NASCAR division that holds races on dirt tracks. Drivers compete in events in several Midwestern states, including Illinois, Iowa, Minnesota, Nebraska, and South Dakota.

8. *Featherlite Southwest Tour.* Brings twenty NASCAR races each year to tracks located primarily in the Southwest. Many of the races are held in combination with Winston Cup and Craftsman Truck races.

9. *Reb-Co Northwest Tour.* Similar to the Featherlite Southwest Tour, except its races are held in the Northwest, primarily in Oregon and Washington. Throughout the year, the Northwest Tour holds races in conjunction with the Southwest Tour and also in combination with the Craftsman Truck series.

10. *Featherlite Modified Tour.* The oldest racing division in NASCAR, and the only touring series that features fenderless (open-wheeled) race cars. Twenty-some races are held in the Northeast, where modified racing has been popular since the 1940s.

11. *Slim Jim All Pro Series.* A series of twenty events that match the country's best short-track racers. Events are held throughout the Southeast as well as in Indiana and Missouri. Many Busch Grand National and Winston Cup drivers began their careers in this series.

12. *Goody's Dash Series.* Considered NASCAR's entry-level touring series, this series features subcompact race cars with powerful four-cylinder engines. There are eighteen races at both short tracks and superspeedways, including an event held in conjunction with the famous Daytona 500.

The Rule Book

All drivers, crews, team owners, and track owners, in order to participate in a NASCAR event, must abide by the rules developed for each racing series. The rule book outlines the procedures for obtaining a membership and a license, and the entry requirements for a race. Race procedures, scoring, and the point system are described in detail. There is a section that covers protests, and one that covers violations and disciplinary actions. But over half of the rule book is devoted to safety and automobile requirements, including five pages of construction guidelines.

NASCAR officials point out that a rule book only sixty pages long is really quite remarkable considering the complexity of motorsports coupled with the challenge of managing a race with forty-two different teams competing simultaneously. In addition, the continual technological breakthroughs require NASCAR's thorough examination. Decisions in this sport occur instantly, and each one must be defensible.

The recipe for NASCAR's success can be found in three simple ingredients: parity, safety, and cost. The rules are the medium for achieving all three.

Five decades of experience have taught NASCAR that lopsided races lead to fan apathy and a drop in gate receipts. The reason 100,000 fans and millions more watching television stay glued to their seat for the entire race is that, until the checkered flag drops, it is still almost anyone's race to win. It is not unusual for a race to end with fifteen cars on the lead lap, separated by less than two or three seconds.

To make sure that the race will be fair, NASCAR requires a series of detailed inspections. Every race has a minimum of three different inspections: prepractice, prequalifying, and prerace. There is a detailed checklist that must be signed by each inspector, acknowledging that the car has met all of the minimum safety standards and regulations. If you are one of the fastest qualifiers, there is an additional inspection, and if you are one of the top four finishers, NASCAR will perform an intensive break-down inspection after the race.

Each year, NASCAR issues rules and regulations for the coming year. It decides which American-made cars are eligible for racing, usually a Buick, Chevrolet, Ford, Mercury, Oldsmobile, and Pontiac model; depending on factory support, however, the racing series will usually settle on just two or three models. Engines approved for racing are standard production-based V8 motors with a minimum displacement of 350 cubic inches and a maximum of 358. The maximum compression limit on any cylinder is 14:1 (compression ratios help determine horsepower). Each engine comes equipped with one four-barrel carburetor.

Cars must weigh a minimum of 3,400 pounds including gas, oil, and water. To ensure parity, each car's weight is adjusted for the weight of its driver. Drivers weighing less than 200 pounds must carry extra weights, in 10-pound increments, up to a maximum of 50 pounds.

The front air dam clearance and rear spoiler of each car are determined by NASCAR; so is the height of each car. Here too, the goal is parity. NASCAR spends a great deal of time in wind-tunnel testing with each model. On average, the distance from the front air dam to the ground is between 3.5 and 4.0 inches. Spoiler heights range from 5.75 to 6.0 inches. The height of each car is set between 50.75 and 51 inches. Each car that seeks to qualify for a race must complete a fifteen-step template test that checks for aerodynamic design of the front, back corners, and sides of the car, including gauges that check the front air dam clearance, the height of the rear spoiler, and the height of the roof line.

The relentlessly detailed inspections are a check for safety, of course, as well as parity. There is another purpose too: to prevent the threat of out-of-control costs. Auto racing, in general, is an expensive sport. To stay viable, NASCAR understands the need to maintain a sensible balance between costs and revenues. NASCAR does not want to see well-financed teams spend thousands of dollars to eke out a tenth of a second of speed. The sanctioning body knows that other less well financed teams, to stay competitive, would have to find a way to meet the challenge, thus racheting the overall cost of racing higher and higher. Furthermore, the concept of rapidly increasing expenses in order to gain an advantage that eventually is neutralized has no utility. Safe, competitive racing at a reasonable cost is the backbone to NASCAR.

The Point System

Each NASCAR racing series uses a point system to determine the series champion. The Winston Cup series point system, although refined over the years, has been in place since 1975. Each NASCAR Winston Cup race, whatever its length or venue, awards the same number of points. The first-place winner receives 175 points, the second-place finisher gets 170 points, and so on down to the fifth-place winner, who gets 155 points. Positions six through ten are separated by four points, and three points separate each finishing position from the eleventh to the last of the field.

The system also includes other bonus points. Each driver can receive five bonus points for leading the race, even if it is only for one lap. A driver can also receive five bonus points for leading the most laps in a race. Bonus points help to create intense racing. Drivers will make a charge for the front to pick up the bonus; once there, they will try to hang on to the lead as long as possible, to earn additional bonus points.

Interesting to note, NASCAR points are awarded to the starting driver of each car, regardless of who is driving at the finish of the race. If a driver has been injured in an earlier race or has become ill, he will often start a race and run a few laps before turning the car over to a relief driver. As long as a driver takes the green flag and completes one lap, he will receive the points earned by the relief driver.

Like the rules and regulations, the point system is designed to keep racing close and competitive. It is to a driver's benefit to be a steady finisher rather than a win-big-or-bust type. A driver who

consistently finishes in the top five will earn more points than a driver who wins a dozen races but fails to finish two dozen.

The point system also helps to ensure that, at each race, all the top drivers will attend. Drivers who are chasing Winston Cup points cannot afford to miss even one race. This is crucial for track owners and promoters, who depend on appearances by big-name drivers to help sell seats.

Breaking the Rules

Section 12 of the racing series rule book covers violations and disciplinary actions. There are thirty different entries in this section, covering membership behavior, inspections, race procedures, and regulations for bodies, parts, equipment, fuel, and tires. Not surprising, because of NASCAR's emphasis on parity and fair play, over half of the violations and penalties cover the car and its equipment. If a NASCAR official determines that an act or omission is sufficiently serious to warrant a penalty, the official notifies the Vice President of Competition, who recommends an appropriate penalty. Penalties include disqualification, probation, suspension of membership, monetary fines, and loss of championship points.

Consistency is a recurring theme in NASCAR, and nowhere is it more apparent than in its behavior toward rule violators. They might be race winners, previous champions, or rising stars; NASCAR shows no favoritism. When seven-time Winston Cup Champion Richard Petty was caught with an illegal engine in 1983, he was fined $35,000 and 104 championship points. In 1995, Jeff Gordon, the series leader and eventual Winston Cup Champion, saw his team fined $60,000 for using an unapproved wheel hub. If a driver gets into a fight with another driver, something that has been known to happen on more than a few occasions, NASCAR will send them both a bill for $10,000.

In addition to NASCAR, another unseen force helps regulate the sport: the financial sponsors. Team members realize that if their sponsor receives negative publicity, either from cheating or boorish behavior, the sponsor may decide to terminate its financial relationship. The fines that NASCAR hands out, although steep, pale in comparison to the risk teams take if they offend their sponsor.

It is impossible to complete a year of racing without some controversy. Ford teams believe Chevrolet teams are given undue advantage and vice versa. Top drivers think the point system works to the disadvantage of race winners. Owners of older tracks worry that they will lose their spots on the racing schedule to newer and more modern super-speedways. Yet, despite the unending debate that surrounds this sport, stock car racing is not only thriving, it is witnessing its fastest growth in history. In a period when fractional interests could easily disrupt the sport, all participants are instead united.

The reason, almost everyone agrees, is that NASCAR has done an outstanding job of managing the sport. Not only has NASCAR proven its ability to enlarge the economic pie, but it has done so in a way that is generally considered to be evenhanded and fair to all. Prosperity does have a way of placating ruffled feathers.

The France Family

Unlike Major League Baseball, the National Football League, or the National Basketball Association, NASCAR is not indirectly owned by its teams. Rather, NASCAR is privately owned by one family, the

France family. For the past fifty years, members of the family have served as the visionaries, the disciplinarians, and the stewards of stock car racing.

Over the years, Bill France's descendants have purchased all the shares of the other three original founding partners; today, NASCAR is 100 percent owned by the France family. Members of the family also own a total of 60 percent of the voting power of International Speedway Corporation. ISC is a publicly traded company (symbol: ISCA—Over the Counter Market) that owns Daytona International Speedway, Talladega Superspeedway, Darlington Raceway, Watkins Glen International Raceway, Tucson Raceway, and Phoenix International Raceway. ISC also owns Motor Racing Network (MRN), Americrown Service Corporation, and DAYTONA USA, a motorsports-themed entertainment complex. In addition, ISC owns 12 percent of Penske Motorsports, which itself owns Michigan Speedway, Nazareth Speedway, North Carolina Motor Speedway (at Rockingham), and the new California Speedway in southern California.

NASCAR is the ultimate family-run business. From 1948 until 1972, the formative years, it was led by Bill France, Sr., with the invaluable behind-the-scenes help of the estimable Annie B. In 1972, France turned the company over to his two sons, Bill and Jim. Under their guidance, stock car racing has become associated with consumer-oriented sponsorship, sophisticated marketing, and national promotion. Today, Bill Jr. is president of NASCAR and has assumed his father's leadership role. Jim is executive vice president of NASCAR and fills the role of chief operating officer; he is also president of ISC. Betty Jane France, Bill's wife, is assistant secretary of NASCAR. Bill and Betty Jane's two children are the third generation of Frances in the business. Brian France is vice president for marketing and corporate communications at NASCAR, and Lesa France Kennedy is executive vice president of International Speedway Corporation and a member of the board of directors.

Bill France, Sr., at six foot five and 240 pounds, was an impressive man. His physical stature and his air of quiet confidence were real assets in the early years, for stock car racing was very much like the Old West—wild and cantankerous. To enforce order and promote stability, stock car racing needed a sheriff, and Big Bill was the perfect lawman.

If asked to describe Bill Sr., most would say he was tough, autocratic, and not afraid to play hardball. Still, he was able to command respect mostly because of his consistency. The rules and regulations of NASCAR, although vigorously enforced, were applied equally. His close friends would also say he was compassionate, even though it was a side that only a few ever saw. But everyone would agree that Bill Sr., more than anything else, was a visionary. Even before there was an organized sport of stock car racing, it was already firmly outlined in his mind. While the sport unfolded and grew, he never wavered from his dream.

In many respects, it was France's wife Annie B who made the dream possible. Where Bill was imposing and charismatic, Annie was calmly competent. Bill was the outspoken public leader; Annie stayed in the background. Throughout the formative NASCAR years, Annie B kept all the books. She was methodical, exacting, and scrupulously precise. Her careful handling of NASCAR's finances matched Bill's consistency in applying the regulations. Together, they created an atmosphere of business integrity that enabled the young organization to thrive.

In the earliest years, there were countless challenges to NASCAR's authority, from fined owners and disqualified drivers, but Bill France never backed down. Even when Richard Petty, the most famous stock car driver ever, organized the Professional Drivers Association (PDA), France would not be intimidated. The PDA boycotted the first race at Talladega, claiming that the tire developed for the track was unsafe. France, at age 59, hopped in a Ford Torino racer and promptly turned a few laps at 176 mph. When the PDA didn't budge, France ran the race anyway with a smaller contingent of NASCAR drivers. The PDA disassembled the following year.

But it wasn't only the drivers and owners that France stared down. When the Automobile Manufacturers Association attempted to outlaw stock car racing because of its inherent dangers, France successfully defused their strategy. When Detroit's manufacturers left the sport because of the public pressure, France funneled money to struggling teams. When the Environmental Protection Agency complained of noise pollution, France countered. When the energy crisis threatened to stop all auto racing, France negotiated to continue by running shorter races. It is generally agreed that France's sheer charisma and unrelenting determination created the sport of stock car racing. His legacy continues to cast a giant shadow over the sport, and the precedents he set are the basis of NASCAR's phenomenal success.

When Bill Sr. passed away on a race-day Sunday morning in 1992, his son William Clifton France, referred to by all as Bill Jr., had already been running NASCAR for twenty years. Many questioned Bill Jr.'s ability; some even predicted NASCAR would start to decline now that Big Bill was gone. They were wrong; NASCAR has not declined on Bill Jr.'s watch, it has exploded.

Bill Sr. brought order to chaos. Bill Jr. is credited with bringing the sport to the level of big business. The timing of the leadership transition was perfect. Having sustained so many tests, NASCAR, by 1972, was firmly entrenched as the undisputed governing body of the sport. What was needed was not a sheriff but an ambassador, someone who knew stock car racing and could communicate its attributes to an increasingly sophisticated audience.

Bill Jr. is the perfect man for the job. He knows the sport of stock car racing inside out, having lived it every day of his life since childhood. And he understands business. Bill Jr. is the consummate business leader. He surrounds himself with top-flight executives and listens carefully to their advice. When all inputs have been considered, he is able to make quick decisions. His subtle demeanor, coupled with a logical approach to problem solving, fits neatly into today's business world. Whereas Bill Sr. breathed life into NASCAR and saw it through its most critical period, Bill Jr. has taken a backwoods regional sport to the national spotlight. While Bill Sr. understood the sport, Bill Jr. understands the product, and that difference has allowed NASCAR to grow to a level some suspect Bill Sr. would have never achieved.

As stock car racing begins its next fifty years, the leadership of NASCAR is stable. Bill Jr. is firmly in control and even at age sixty-five shows no signs of slowing down. Jim France, his younger brother, is a proficient businessman and possesses the same subtle approach to solving business problems as does Bill Jr. His demeanor is quiet, steady, precise. In personality and workstyle, he reminds many people of Annie B. So, in the same way that Big Bill and Annie B made a strong team because of their complementary styles, their two sons have linked their skills and styles to invigorate the business.

Bill Jr.'s children, Brian and Lesa, represent NASCAR's third generation; already they are demonstrating the skills necessary to lead stock car racing in the next century. It is not an exaggeration to say that the third-generation thinking is what has catapulted NASCAR to prominence. Bill Sr. thought of stock car racing as a sport; Bill Jr.

saw it as a product; Brian and Lesa have extended the concept even further: they refer to it as an entertainment product. The difference reflects a carefully planned shift in company strategy.

Making the shift did not come easily to Bill Jr. Brian France, and his aggressive marketing group, constantly pestered Bill Jr. to broaden his thinking. Bill often responded by asking for more information, more research. Brian persevered. He knew that NASCAR was entertainment, and that providing entertainment afforded many more opportunities than simply sanctioning races.

Over the past few years, NASCAR has become a marketing powerhouse. There is a NASCAR Website. There are NASCAR magazines and newspapers. There are NASCAR videos and television programs. There are NASCAR flags, shirts, mugs, and car products; the licensing extensions, in fact, are almost endless.

The genius of the current crop of Frances is taking the NASCAR name beyond licensed products, into the kinds of brand extensions that are available only to entertainment-type companies. When NASCAR opened a retail store called NASCAR Thunder, Brian will tell you that his model was the Warner Brothers retail stores. When NASCAR opened a restaurant called the NASCAR Café, they will tell you that the model was the Hard Rock Café. When Lesa Kennedy tackled the spectacular interactive DAYTONA USA, they knew the model was Walt Disney World.

NASCAR has come a long way from the days of dirt tracks and hell-raisin' drivers. Today, it is a sports entertainment business on a scale comparable to any other major sports organization. NASCAR's licensing program, particularly its stores, restaurants, and speedparks, is extending the NASCAR brand into nonrace markets. These innovative marketing ventures attract not only new fans, but younger fans who will provide the base for continuing nationwide support for stock car racing.

The focus of NASCAR'S marketing effort is promoting the sport not only for itself, but for track owners and teams. Some business observers might scratch their heads at this approach, but it is very difficult to argue with success. The underlying strength of NASCAR is tied to its continuing mission to provide financial stability for all participants, not just for itself. It was the basis of Bill France Sr.'s philosophy when he organized NASCAR, it became the cornerstone for Bill Jr.'s management, and it will continue to be the key for Brian France and Lesa Kennedy as they drive the sport into the next century.

3

IT TAKES MONEY
TO RACE

IN 1951, DETROIT'S Chamber of Commerce was busily preparing to celebrate the city's 250th anniversary. The planners had scheduled a long list of festivities, but still they felt something was lacking. Then Big Bill France called with an intriguing proposal. What the Motor City's anniversary needed, he said, was an auto race. It would be the ideal event for a city known as the automobile capital of the world.

Bill France knew a good opportunity when he saw it. Located within the Michigan State Fairgrounds was a one-mile dirt racetrack. The race he envisioned would run for 250 miles—one mile for each of Detroit's 250 years. Then, as part of his campaign to make the race a success, France, the seasoned race promoter, contacted all the automobile manufacturers and asked them to enter at least one of their cars in the race. Up to that time, auto manufacturers hadn't paid much attention to stock car racing, but Bill France was a hard person to say no to.

47

On the afternoon of August 12, a crowd of 16,500 fans filled the track to capacity to watch the start of the "Motor City 250." Sprinkled throughout the grandstands, notable in their coats and ties, were the executives of fifteen different auto manufacturers. For the next four hours, they stood and watched with amazement.

The Motor City 250 was the perfect race to showcase NASCAR's talents. The fifty-nine-car field provided nonstop excitement. The lead changed fourteen times and wasn't settled until Tommy Thompson, driving a '51 Chrysler, outwitted Joe Eubanks and his '50 Oldsmobile 88 on the last lap.

The most anticipated event of the celebration was a huge success, and Detroit's Chamber of Commerce was ecstatic. "Stock Car racing, NASCAR style, was a big hit in the Motor City," read the headline.[1] Big Bill France had succeeded again. In one bold stroke, he accomplished two significant events. First, stock car racing, a southern-bred sport, had found acceptance north of the Mason–Dixon line. Second, and more important, France had introduced stock car racing to Detroit's skeptical auto makers and had won them over.

Stock car racing, like motorsports in general, is an expensive undertaking. In the early years—before television, licensing ventures, and sophisticated corporate sponsorships—stock car drivers lived from race to race, scrambling to find ways to cover the cost of an automobile, replacement parts, mechanical overhauls, tires, gasoline, salaries for the crew, and traveling expenses. Although the total race purse at each track was on the rise, individual winnings were still well below the cost of fielding a race team.

At the Motor City 250, for example, the first-place prize was $5,000; second-place, $2,000; and third-place, $1,000. But fourth place through tenth place won only a few hundred dollars, and the rest of the finishers took home between $25 and $50. With the exception of the top few finishers, drivers at the Motor City 250 didn't cover the cost of racing; many didn't even cover the cost of a set of tires. Bill France knew that if stock car racing was to survive, it would need not only an expanding fan base but immediate financial support.

Fifty years ago, there was no concept of corporate sponsorship for sporting events. When Bill France first approached automobile and tire manufacturers and gasoline companies to ask them to invest in stock car racing, it was out of financial necessity. France instinctively knew that these types of companies were ideal prospects for NASCAR, and indeed Chevrolet, Ford, Goodyear, and Unocal have all been outstanding partners with stock car racing for much of NASCAR's fifty-year history. But little did France know that by reaching out to major corporations and asking for their help, he was in fact trailblazing what has become today the most sophisticated type of marketing—corporate sponsorship.

The Sponsorship Philosophy

Sponsorship is a form of marketing in which companies attach their name, brand, or logo to an event for the purpose of achieving future profits. It is not the same as advertising. Both strategies seek the same end result—corporate profit—but go about it in different ways. Advertising is a direct and overt message to consumers. If successful, it stimulates a near-term purchase. Sponsorship, on the other hand, generates a more subtle message that, if successful, creates a lasting bond between consumers and the company.

How important is sponsorship in the field of marketing? According to *IEG Sponsorship Report*, a Chicago-based newsletter that covers sports, arts, and special-event marketing, U.S. companies will spend almost $6 billion on sponsorship in North America in 1997. More importantly, in the five-year period from 1993 through 1997, corporate spending on sponsorship increased more than 13 percent each year. During the same period, advertising spending grew, on average, 7 percent annually, and sales promotion (a third strategy) increased by only 5 percent each year.

Clearly, there has been a pronounced shift in marketing dollars toward sponsorship. Today, over fifty companies spend more than $10 million annually on sponsorship programs, and several major corporations invest upward of $100 million:

Philip Morris	$125 million
Anheuser-Busch	120
The Coca-Cola Company	95
General Motors Corporation	75
PepsiCo	65
AT&T	55
Eastman Kodak	50
RJR Nabisco	50
Chrysler Corporation	40
McDonald's	40

These dollar amounts are for sponsorship deals only and do not include additional money that is spent on advertising, promotion, and client entertainment.

Why have corporations begun to shift so much of their marketing resources into sponsorship programs? Impact. In an era when the consumer is overwhelmed with advertising messages, sponsorship is a way to distinguish a company's message to a captured audience.

Not all sponsorship dollars are invested in sports, but sporting events do represent the most significant portion. Out of $6 billion in sponsorship dollars in 1997, 65 percent—$3.9 billion—was earmarked for sports. Entertainment tours and attractions take 11 percent of the sponsorship pie, festival and fairs get 9 percent, special causes get another 9 percent, and 6 percent is spent on art events.

We should not be surprised that sporting events garner the largest segment of sponsorship dollars. The enormous audience size—attendees plus television viewers—makes sports events attractive for sponsors. But what is surprising to many observers is that, within the sports event category, stock car racing, compared to football, basketball, baseball, and even the Olympics, is providing the highest return for its sponsorship dollars—a fact that is no longer lost on Madison Avenue.

Making the Most of a Sponsorship Investment

Despite the rapidly growing investment in sponsorship marketing, the strategy still suffers from two widely held misperceptions. One is the belief that sponsorship involves nothing more than placing a name on a banner and then displaying that banner conspicuously. Second, although most people admit that sponsorship does carry some benefit, many still believe that its results cannot be measured. Both of these beliefs are largely untrue.

Leveraging the Impact

It is theoretically possible to put up money to sponsor an event, hang a big billboard at the event, and have that be the end of it. But any organization that looked on sponsorship in this limited fashion would be foolish indeed. As with any other business investment, the resources devoted to sponsorship pay off fully only when they are intelligently leveraged.

We know that sponsorship works to highlight a company in what is otherwise a vat of indistinguishable media messages. Sponsorship, overall, does increase corporate visibility. Each time a company's logo or name is seen by consumers attending the event (or watching it on television), an impression is created. To take full advantage of those impressions, most companies link their sponsorship and advertising programs, so that each reinforces the other.

In stock car racing, the corporate role is, by tradition, given great prominence. If a company sponsors a racing event, the company's name is incorporated into the event name. For example, Mountain Dew, one of PepsiCo's many soft drinks, sponsors Darlington's Southern 500 race. Hence, the race itself is known as the Mountain Dew Southern 500. If a company becomes a team sponsor, the corporate name or brand is used in conjunction with the team name. Rick Hendrick owns a car sponsored by Kellogg's and Chevrolet and driven by Terry Labonte. In referring to the team and its race car, commentators and fans alike talk about Labonte's Kellogg's Chevrolet Monte Carlo. And both Kellogg's and Chevrolet develop national advertising campaigns that feature their car and winning driver in the ads. That's leverage.

Many companies use their sponsorship association to develop a distinct corporate image. Racing is viewed as a fast, tough, exciting, innovative, and aggressive sport, and many companies are finding out that being linked to those qualities gives them distinct marketing advantages. Additionally, companies use their sponsorship of racing for other promotional tie-ins. Whether tied directly to a track or to the surrounding region during a race weekend, these promotions are a way for companies to call attention to their sponsorship and, by extension, their products. For example, in the spring of 1997, Heilig-Meyers, a Charlotte furniture retailer that sponsors a Winston Cup team, offered a 10 percent discount on purchases to customers who brought in a ticket stub from a Charlotte race; that offer was announced over the public address system, on radio spots, and on billboards near the track. Each time the special offer was mentioned or seen, the Heilig-Meyers name was reinforced in the minds of the fans.

There are also several spinoff benefits associated with sponsorship; two noteworthy ones are opportunities for corporate entertainment and ways to increase employee morale. Companies that sponsor racing find the association has an overall positive effect on their workers, from the executive offices down to the assembly line. To further stimulate employee performance, many companies instigate awards programs based on meeting sales goals, reducing absentee rates, or increasing productivity. The winners of these programs are treated to a corporate adventure that naturally includes a weekend at the races.

Corporate entertainment has increasingly become an effective marketing tool, both for solidifying relationships with valuable customers and for wooing new ones. When stock car racing becomes part of the entertainment package, the results can be impressive. A sponsor's guests are given a guided tour through the pit area and garage, and often get an opportunity to meet and talk with a driver. After a reception in the sponsor's elegant hospitality tent, guests are escorted to VIP grandstand seats. By the time the checkered flag drops, even the most buttoned-down business executive can't help but be caught up in the excitement.

DuPont, which sponsors Jeff Gordon's DuPont Chevrolet Monte Carlo team, one of three Winston Cup teams owned by

Rick Hendrick, is a master at making the most of its sponsorship. At each Winston Cup race, DuPont entertains anywhere between 400 and 2,000 guests, clients, and employees. A typical race weekend includes an elaborate breakfast at the hospitality tent, a meeting with Jeff Gordon, a tour of the pit and garage area, and premium seats from which to watch the race.

Gatorade, one of the first nonautomotive companies to sponsor NASCAR racing (beginning in 1977), brings corporate executives and VIP guests to its hospitality suite, and even holds its sales meetings at the track on a race weekend, to invigorate the sales force. Gatorade, the perennial sponsor of all manner of sporting events, takes full advantage of its NASCAR sponsorship, and considers it a good investment. "If I had an additional marketing dollar to allocate," says Bill Schmidt, marketing vice president, "I would spend it on NASCAR."[2]

It is perhaps valuable to remind ourselves here that the fundamental reason companies invest in sponsorships is to increase profits. The companies that have been most successful in doing so are the ones that have included all these marketing strategies in conjunction with their sponsorship. That means that the cost of a successful sponsorship includes not only the price of the sponsorship itself but the cost of additional advertising, promotions, and entertainment. Some have suggested that to receive the full benefit of sponsorship, a company should be willing to spend at least an additional dollar on marketing tie-ins for every dollar spent on sponsorship.

This does not mean, however, that sponsorship is limited to companies with huge budgets. On the contrary, as we will learn, a great advantage of NASCAR is the various financial levels it makes available for sponsorship. What it does mean is that a sponsoring company that uses its name at an event and does nothing else, is not going to receive the full benefit for its marketing dollars.

Measuring the Impact

Despite its unequivocal success as a marketing tool, no one can unequivocally state the absolute, to-the-decimal benefit that companies receive for their sponsorship dollars. Because the greatest benefit of sponsorship is the residual value of accumulated consumer biases that are created over time, calculating the precise dollar value at any given point is difficult. Still, companies, event organizers, and marketing executives are working hard to create a standardized method for calculating returns for sponsorship events.

The challenge of measuring returns is made easier when companies first outline their reasons for the sponsorship. If the goal is simply to increase sales, the sales figures from a sponsorship period are easily compared with other periods when sponsorship was not used. If a company goal is to reduce employee absenteeism or to increase productivity, and if the company rewards results with some benefit tied to sponsorship, the effect of sponsorship is easy enough to measure. What was the absenteeism rate with and without sponsorship-related benefits? What productivity increases can be attributed to a sponsorship benefit period? Similarly, the sponsorship benefits of entertainment programs are simple to measure. Did the clients who attended a race increase their orders relative to other clients who were not invited? Did entertaining prospects at a race event create more client conversions than occurred among other prospects?

These kinds of sponsorship activities lend themselves to quantification. The investment required to achieve new sales or acquire new

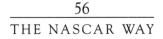
clients can be measured and is known by most companies. Likewise, most companies know the cost of absenteeism and the value of productivity gains. Hence, it is not complicated to figure whether the cost of sponsorship, a fixed dollar amount, is a profitable investment relative to increasing sales, acquiring new clients, reducing absenteeism, or heightening productivity.

The difficulty in measuring the benefits of sponsorship comes not from specific goals like sales and new accounts, but from the more elusive goal of enhancing corporate images. To what degree do consumers have a more positive outlook toward companies that sponsor stock car racing compared to other companies that do not? To what degree is placing a corporate logo on a race car a better investment than advertising on television, radio, and billboards, and in newspapers or magazines?

The science of measuring corporate images is still evolving. However, indications point to overwhelming acceptance and positive consumer support for companies that sponsor the sport of stock car racing. The evidence is even more dramatic when the sponsorship returns for stock car racing are compared to those for football, basketball, baseball, soccer, hockey, golf, tennis, or the Olympics.

Measuring the Emotional Impact

Are those 180-mph rolling billboards really worth what a sponsorship costs? Wouldn't a company be better off investing that money in more traditional advertising vehicles, like print and broadcast media? The proponents of sponsorship strategies are constantly asked these questions. It is not surprising that they turn first to a statistical defense.

Joyce Julius and Associates, of Ann Arbor, Michigan, tracks sponsors' exposure at events and publishes the results in the widely respected *The Sponsor's Report.* Using a battalion of statisticians and television sets all tuned to the same event, Joyce Julius tallies the number of times a sponsor's name is mentioned in a broadcast and computes the sponsor's in-focus TV exposure time. When a television camera zooms in for three seconds on Labonte's Kellogg's Chevrolet Monte Carlo racing around the track, Joyce Julius puts a dollar value on that opportunity, based on the cost of buying three seconds of advertising during the race.

The idea is that sponsors will use this measuring stick to gauge their return on their marketing investment. If, at the end of the season, the sponsorship dollars have generated free mentions or exposures valued higher than what those dollars could have purchased in commercial time, the investment is profitable.

Can we assume that multiple brief exposures over a three-hour race carry as much weight as a full commercial? Skeptics would argue they do not. Proponents, on the other hand, would argue that these split-second exposures are actually more valuable since most people, during commercials, either leave the room for a quick break or become easily distracted with conversation. To avoid any concern, sponsors that use the Joyce Julius numbers often apply a multiple. If the exposure time provided by the sponsorship is three to five times greater than the advertising time those dollars would purchase, the investment is deemed wise.

But quantifying television exposure tells us only part of the story. What sponsoring companies are quickly learning is that the real value of stock car racing comes not from the impressions of additional exposures, but from the emotions the impressions generate.

Stock car racing is about impact. It is impossible to attend a race without being overwhelmed. The sound of forty-two 700-horsepower engines hidden below an amazing tapestry of brightly colored race cars creates emotion. Once these lightning-quick cars begin racing each other, adrenaline soon works to heighten the overall effect. The inevitable collisions that occur during a race produce intense spikes of both excitement and fear.

But do these emotions translate to a positive corporate image? Is sponsoring stock car racing more or less effective than sponsoring other types of sports? And does sponsorship contribute to the underlying goal of corporate profits? As you would imagine, companies spend a great deal of time and effort trying to answer these questions. Increasing sales, adding new accounts, and reducing absenteeism all lend themselves to quantitative tests. Image perception is more difficult to quantify.

Survey research is the most common way to measure image perception. The person holding a clipboard, who walks up to you and asks whether you have a minute to answer a few questions, is conducting a survey. Companies often survey fans before and after a race, sometimes supplementing the responses with telephone interviews a few days later.

Sponsoring companies carefully guard their survey results. They have no interest in sharing with competitors the returns generated from their sponsorship programs. But it is clear that something positive is at work in this sport. Simple testaments are: the strong growth in the number of new sponsors, and the increasing financial commitment of existing sponsors.

To date, the hardest research results available on the effectiveness of sponsoring stock car racing come not from a sponsor but from an independent research observer. Because of the number of calls it received about NASCAR and stock car racing, Performance Research, a sports marketing research firm in Newport, Rhode Island, decided to conduct its own in-depth study on this sport. The results, published in a 1994 report called *RaceStat*, provided corporate sponsors with an objective view of NASCAR and its audience. What Performance Research learned has stunned the marketing world. The research has enlightened major corporations to the opportunities and benefits in NASCAR and has served as a wake-up call to the other national sports programs.

Performance Research's *RaceStat* study revealed two important facts about NASCAR. First, stock car racing fans are very aware of who sponsors their sport, and second, they have a strong tendency to purchase the products of sponsoring companies. Performance Research surveyed 1,000 NASCAR fans and asked them to identify which companies sponsored stock car racing. Respondents were able to identify, without aid, more than 200 companies or brands connected to the sport. They were able to identify a car's sponsor most easily; event and series sponsors were less well remembered.

Of all the companies mentioned as sponsors, only 1 percent were incorrectly named. This is an extraordinary level of awareness. For comparison, consider that, in 1992, Visa Credit Card paid $20 million to become the official sponsor of the Winter and Summer Olympics. A follow-up survey conducted by Performance Research found that 30 percent of the respondents believed American Express was the official sponsor.[3]

Not only are stock car fans aware of which companies sponsor their sport, they are fiercely loyal to those companies. Performance Research discovered that three out of four stock car racing fans consciously purchase products of NASCAR sponsors. In comparison, only half of tennis fans and golf fans have that same loyalty. As for the fans of Major League Baseball, the National Basketball Association, and the National Football League, the Performance Research results indicate that roughly one in three—less than half the rate of NASCAR fans—purchase the products of their sport's sponsors.

The testimony does not end here. It was further revealed in the survey that NASCAR fans have a higher level of trust toward race

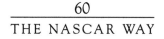

sponsors' products—approximately 60 percent of the respondents, compared to only 30 percent of football fans. Finally, in what may be a sponsor's ultimate goal, over 40 percent of NASCAR's fans purposely switched brands when a manufacturer became a NASCAR sponsor.

Their brand awareness, trust in sponsoring companies, conscious purchase of the products of NASCAR sponsors, and willingness to switch to products of the sport's new sponsors would seem to indicate that NASCAR fans are unique in the sporting world. Is it possible that NASCAR fans are simply more loyal, more attentive than other sports fans? On the contrary, "NASCAR fans are not genetically predisposed to sponsor loyalty," argues Lesa Ukman, co-founder of *IEG Sponsorship Report*. Rather, "NASCAR has just done an extraordinary job of educating them [fans] as to the sponsor's importance to the sport."[4]

Since birth, NASCAR has understood how expensive it is to participate in stock car racing. Whereas baseball, football, and basketball all started with a fairly low operating base, which allowed owners to make a decent profit on their investment, the sport of stock car racing began with a substantial financial burden. In order to survive, the sport had to master the sponsorship relationship. Today's fans know how important the sponsors are; so do the drivers.

"Motorsports lends itself to sponsorship because it is a very expensive sport," explains T. Wayne Robertson, senior vice president of sports marketing for RJR Nabisco.[5] Fans realize that, without corporate sponsorship, the ticket prices for races would be substantially higher. Drivers are acutely aware, and so are fans, that without corporate sponsorship teams would not be able to race.

When Geoff Bodine wrecked his QVC Ford Thunderbird in the early laps of the 1996 Daytona 500, he used some of the time during a television interview to apologize to the fans and to his sponsor.

Not only was he sorry for depriving his team of the opportunity to complete the famous Daytona 500, but he was equally sorry for depriving QVC's employees, friends, and customers of the opportunity to see their race car in action. What Bodine did next neatly summarizes the relationship between stock car racing and its sponsors. Before the interview ended, he turned to the camera and told his fans to "call the QVC shopping channel and order some more merchandise because we are going to need to build a new car."

Affordable, Flexible Sponsorship

Some companies may look at NASCAR and conclude that because they are not Fortune 500 corporations they are not financially equipped to be sponsors. But a NASCAR sponsorship does not always involve a significant investment, and the notion that any company's marketing budget is too small is generally rebuked by NASCAR. Even if the budget is only several thousand dollars, it is likely that NASCAR can find a way to help the company become a sponsor for the sport.

First of all, NASCAR's twelve racing divisions offer companies different economic levels at which to participate. Naturally, to become a sponsor at the Winston Cup level would require a larger investment than for the other racing series. However, the Busch Grand National division and the Craftsman Truck series offer companies national television exposure at sponsorship rates significantly lower than those for the Winston Cup, and the Winston West series or the Busch North series costs even less.

Second, within each series, there is a wide range of sponsorship options, grouped into these distinct categories: NASCAR sponsorship, event sponsorship, and team sponsorship.

NASCAR Sponsorship

If a company wants to spread its marketing dollars over the widest possible area, a sponsorship dedicated to the sport itself is the right approach. Four separate NASCAR sponsorship programs are available for companies: Official Status, Series Sponsorship, Special Awards Program, and NASCAR Online.

1. The NASCAR *Official Status* program elevates a sponsor to the highest level. Official Status sponsors can use the NASCAR name and logo to help advertise their products. PepsiCo, as an official NASCAR sponsor, is allowed to include the NASCAR brand in its own product advertising and at the same time declare itself "the Official Soft Drink of NASCAR." Kodak is an official sponsor of NASCAR and thus becomes "the Official Film and One-Time-Use Camera of NASCAR." Busch is the "Official Beer," Raybestos is the "Official Brake," and Opryland USA is the "Official Destination of NASCAR."

The investment required to become an Official Status sponsor is significant. The price tag varies according to the size of a company, its total revenues, and the percentage of its revenues relevant to stock car racing, but, generally speaking, it's around $1.5 million a year. (A national sponsorship with Major League Baseball costs approximately the same; with the National Basketball Association, the tab is $2.8 million; with the National Football League, $4.5 million.[6]) NASCAR doesn't keep the full $1.5 million. About 25 percent of it goes into the Winston Cup Championship fund, and thus ultimately back to the competitors.

2. *Series Sponsorship* allows a company to use its name to identify a racing series. Anheuser-Busch pays NASCAR for the opportunity to put its name on the Grand National series, now called the

"Busch Grand National series." Similarly, Featherlite Trailers sponsors the "Featherlite Modified Tour" and Slim Jim underwrites the "Slim Jim All-Pro Series." RJR Nabisco Company has sponsored NASCAR's premier series since 1972. For that privilege, the company renamed the series the "Winston Cup," after Winston cigarettes, one of its brands.

This category of sponsorship requires the largest investment. Each year, RJR Nabisco pays $30 million for this distinction: approximately $4 million to $5 million in cash, with the balance dedicated to advertising and promoting NASCAR.[7]

3. Becoming a series sponsor or an Official Status sponsor is a significant investment. However, becoming a NASCAR sponsor is not limited to the millionaire's club. The *Special Awards Program* provides companies an opportunity to tap NASCAR's fan base by presenting cash awards linked to the performance of drivers, crew chiefs, and crew members.

True Value Hardware Stores sponsors the $50,000 True Value Hard Charger Award. At the end of the year, the three drivers who drove the most miles up front share the award and prize money. Western Auto sponsors the $25,000 Mechanic of the Year Award. RCA sponsors the $50,000 Pit Strategy Award, honoring the year's top crew chief. Busch Beer sponsors the Busch Pole Award, a cash prize for the fastest qualifier for each individual race. Gatorade provides a $10,000 Front Runner Award for the team that is leading at the halfway point, and Unocal gives a prize for any team that is both the fastest qualifier and the race winner. MCI pays the $5,000 "Fast Pace" award to the driver who records the fastest lap speed while leading the race. There is even an award for the driver who suffers the worst luck during a race: the "Headache Award," from Goody's Headache Powders. The total value of these awards is not insignificant. At the 1996 Daytona 500, special awards totaled $1.5 million.

In all cases, to be eligible for the prizes, the teams must be willing to place the company's decal on the side of the race car. Thus, the Special Awards sponsors get a valuable extra benefit: race-day exposure. The kaleidoscope of corporate emblems that wrap the front quarter panel of a stock car are decals either paid for by direct sponsors of the race team (described below) or placed on the car by the team so as to qualify for the special cash prizes.

4. *NASCAR Online* is NASCAR's Internet site on the World Wide Web (www.nascar.com). By using NASCAR Online, race fans are treated to daily updates about teams, drivers, and the sport of stock car racing. On race weekends, it is not uncommon for the Website to receive well over one million hits. Race fans are able to receive real-time results on qualifying runs as well as ongoing standings during the race. Recently, *NASCAR Winston Cup Scene* and *NASCAR Winston Cup Illustrated,* a weekly newspaper and a monthly periodical, both owned by Street & Smith's Sports Publication, began offering selected articles for the Website.

NASCAR Online offers several unique sponsorship advantages. First, whereas other Websites might include two or three sponsors on a single page, NASCAR limits the exposure to one. Currently, NASCAR Online includes five sponsors; each gets full-page exposure, in rotation with the others. Unlike race events, where there is a great deal of signage, NASCAR Online offers the opportunity to focus on a particular sponsor.

Generally, the sponsors of NASCAR Online are also sponsors of the sport. For example, Kodak, Budweiser, and McDonald's sponsor race teams and also are Website sponsors. Most of them further integrate the NASCAR fan with online promotional events. Kodak sponsors a photo-of-the-month contest; Budweiser sponsors a trivia game. But it is not only traditional NASCAR sponsors that are benefiting from NASCAR Online. Microsoft, while marketing its Internet browser called Explorer, turned to NASCAR Online. "The beauty of NASCAR," explains Shelley Morrison, director of advertising at Starwave Corporation, the leading Internet site developer, "is that you get passionate 'wired' fans."[8]

NASCAR Online provides individual advertising banners across its thirty pages of information. Each sponsor rotates to a front page where a hot-link logo connects NASCAR fans with the sponsor's own Website. NASCAR Online generates over 22 million hits among 500,000 different users each week. With sponsorship rates at $15,000 per month or $120,000 per year, NASCAR Online guarantees the sponsors 300,000 impressions per month. Already, these numbers are rising. "That is one of the nice things about NASCAR Online," points out Morrison; "the growth potential is huge."

Event Sponsorship

Sponsoring one specific event, one race in a series, is an ideal strategy for promoting a brand on a regional basis. No matter what level of national television or press coverage any individual race receives, the fans attending the event—who, we can presume, come mostly from the general area—receive a barrage of sponsor messages, both verbal and visual, as part of the day's happenings. The 75,000 fans who happily squeeze into Darlington Raceway for the Southern 500 hear the phrase "Mountain Dew Southern 500" countless times before the day is over.

One hundred NASCAR racetracks are in use across the country, including twenty that host a Winston Cup race. Although most of the tracks are located in the Southeast, not all of them are limited to this geographic area. Sponsors with regional marketing plans can also target northern California (there is a Winston Cup track in San Francisco), Arizona (Phoenix), upstate New York (Watkins Glen), or New Hampshire (Concord). In 1997, two new tracks opened, one in Texas (Dallas–Fort Worth) and one in southern California (Fontana, outside Los Angeles). It is predicted that future Winston Cup race dates will be hosted in other areas outside the southeastern corridor, so that, in the years to come, a sponsor will be able to select any major regional area in the country.

The cost to sponsor a Winston Cup event varies according to the size of the event and the size of the marketing region. PepsiCo pays approximately $1 million for each Mountain Dew Southern 500 race. The Coca-Cola Company sponsors a series of events at Charlotte Motor Speedway during the month of May, including the Coca-Cola 600, the longest Winston Cup race of the year. Coca-Cola will not say how much this sponsorship costs, but several million dollars would be a fair guess.

The company has no doubt it gets its money's worth. According to Michael Guth, Brand Manager Executive at Coca-Cola, sponsorship of the Winston Cup race "is one of the most productive expenditures the company has ever made to promote the soft drink brand." When asked why Coca-Cola has dedicated so much effort and money to sponsor Winston Cup racing, Guth has two quick answers: (1) "Consumers have an intense passion for this sport." (2) "There is a tremendous trust and respect for the sponsors involved in the sport."[9]

NASCAR Winston Cup races are the most expensive because they pull the biggest audiences, but companies without million-dollar budgets can still tap into the local fan base by sponsoring a race in one of the other NASCAR series. Often, a speedway will schedule a Busch series race or a Craftsman Truck series race on the Saturday before Sunday's Winston Cup race. The cost for one of these support races is significantly less than sponsorship of a Winston Cup race: approximately $500,000 for a Busch race, and between $200,000 and $250,000 for a truck race.

There is one other way for companies to associate themselves with an event and reach the local fans: by purchasing advertising space in the event program. This is not sponsorship in the strict sense of the word, but it is a relatively low-cost marketing strategy that puts the company's message right in the lap of the fans. A full-page ad in a Winston Cup event program costs around $3,500; a half-page ad is $2,000.

Team Sponsorship

The premier sponsorship available in NASCAR is team sponsorship. It is the most valuable because it allows a company to take a direct equity participation in the sport. Only in stock car racing is this possible, and it is one of the aspects of this sport that makes it supremely interesting to marketing professionals.

A team sponsor is allowed to put the company name, logo, or brand directly on the car and on the uniforms of the driver and crew members. This is not at all the same as the Nike swoosh on the shoes of an NBA player, or the discreet Speedo logo on the swimwear of the U.S. Diving team. The entire surface of a stock car, except the roof and doors, is covered with sponsors' insignia in various sizes. The primary sponsor gets the most prominent space, of course. Perhaps even more important, it gets total identification with the race team.

The company name, the race team, the driver, and the car itself are fully and indelibly linked together. In the minds of fans, they are one and the same. Terry Labonte's car is Kellogg's car. Jeff Gordon's car is the DuPont car, Dale Earnhardt drives the Goodwrench car, and the Tide car belongs to Ricky Rudd. Ask any person at a race-track, "Who's your favorite driver?" and then ask, "Who sponsors him?" You will *always* get the right answer. Or pick any fan at random, mention the name of a sponsor, and that fan can, without hesitation, name the driver. The emotional bond that exists between fans and corporate sponsors in stock car racing is unlike any other in the world of sport.

How much does it cost to sponsor a team? The amount can vary, depending on the team's performance history and its expected success. Teams that have a history of finishing high in the Winston Cup standings command more money, and teams that have shown mediocre results in the past can be sponsored for less. However, a new team that boasts a well-known driver and an experienced crew chief may cost a sponsor as much as an established successful team.

The price tag for sponsoring a Winston Cup team starts at $1.5 million per season. To sponsor a team that has a history of finishing the year in the top twenty, the cost is approximately $5 million a season. If you want to sponsor the best race teams in the Winston Cup series, including the teams at Richard Childress Racing, Robert Yates Racing, or Hendrick Motorsports, be prepared to pay between $5 million and $10 million per year.

Each stock car is a corporate billboard, literally. Except for the doors and roof, where NASCAR rules permit only the team number, every available inch of space on a car is reserved for a sponsor. Every NASCAR Winston Cup race is nationally televised, giving the sponsors a three-hour revolving advertising sign.

Team sponsors use the high visibility of race cars to give special plugs to new products. When Procter & Gamble wants to promote a new brand, Ricky Rudd's Thunderbird is painted to reflect the product. When Kellogg's wants to introduce a new cereal, Terry Labonte's

Monte Carlo gets the nod. When Jeff Gordon ran the 1997 Winston Select, an all-star race at Charlotte, his DuPont Chevrolet sported a flashy new design. Painted bright red with dinosaur decals, it became the Jurassic Park car, promoting the Jurassic Park ride at Universal Studios.

As with other categories of sponsorship, companies interested in team sponsorship have a range of opportunities. The hood and the rear quarter panels are reserved for the primary sponsor and usually cost between $3 million and $6 million a season. The primary sponsor may take the entire area, or the area may be sold as a package that includes secondary sponsors. The trunk lid, called the TV panel because it can be seen from other drivers' in-car cameras, is available for $500,000 to $1 million, and is often included in the hood/quarter-panel package.

For $250,000 to $750,000, a sponsor can place its name behind the back tires or on the C-Post, which is the side area next to the back window. The B-Post, the side area next to the driver's window, costs approximately $200,000 for the season.

For smaller investments, companies can participate in the decal program. Rectangular decals with a company's name or logo, designed to be displayed on the sides of the cars, come in two basic sizes. At the Winston Cup level, a twenty-six-inch decal costs a company approximately $2,000 per race with a minimum posting of thirty-two races, which brings the advertising investment to $64,000. For a thirty-two-inch decal, the cost is $2,500 per race, or $80,000.

The race car is not the only area where a team's sponsorship appears. Today, a driver and his crew are smartly outfitted in racing uniforms every bit as brightly decorated as the team's car. Sponsors negotiate not only the price and area where the company's name will appear on the race car, but also the area where the name appears on the team's uniforms.

Attaching a corporate name directly on a uniform is not a revolutionary concept in sports marketing. To a lesser degree, tennis and golf have come to accept corporate emblems on players' clothing. But no sport can match the blatant sponsorship of stock car racing. Because sponsorship is so much a part of racing's heritage, no one gives a second thought to seeing corporate emblems pasted everywhere in this sport. In fact, a car and race team that shows up at a track without a primary sponsor is often embarrassed.

Sponsoring a NASCAR Winston Cup team is the most expensive investment, with the exception of a series sponsorship, that a company can make in stock car racing. However, the price tag is justifiable, considering the payback the sponsor receives. Some have even argued that sponsoring a Winston Cup race team is one of the last marketing bargains available in sports.

What is the value of placing a corporate name directly on a team in a sport that is as widely followed and appreciated as NASCAR? Imagine for a moment the hypothetical value of sponsoring the New York Yankees, the Dallas Cowboys, or the Chicago Bulls. How much would IBM pay to see the team become the IBM Yankees? How much would Coca-Cola pay to create the Coca-Cola Cowboys; or United Airlines, the United Bulls?

DuPont, which sponsors the Jeff Gordon team at Hendrick Motorsports, has enthusiastically embraced the sport of stock car racing. Gordon, a former Winston Cup Champion, is one of the fastest rising stars in stock car racing, and his team is one of the most expensive. DuPont monitors every event and tracks its sales from the racing sponsorship. "It gives us the chance to get closer to our customers, and sales increase as a result," explains Tom Speakman, marketing manager at DuPont. But have the millions invested in stock car racing paid off? "Let me put it this way," Speakman says, "we're very comfortable with the return on our investment."[10]

Sponsorship on the Pacific Rim

In 1996, NASCAR created a new avenue for sponsorship expansion with its first exhibition race in Japan. At the inaugural Suzuka Circuit race, Japanese race fans came out in droves. NASCAR and its stars returned to Suzuka again in 1997, and in 1998 they will race at the new Twin Ring Motegi track, seventy miles northwest of Tokyo. It is the largest private construction project in Japanese history, built at a cost of $400 million. Ironically, the oval-designed track turned into an egg shape just like Darlington.

Is NASCAR envisioning an international racing series? Not really. "We certainly don't expect the NASCAR Winston Cup series will turn into a series of international events," says Paul Brooks, NASCAR's director of special projects. "However, in the long term, we do envision a NASCAR series in Japan with Japanese teams and Japanese drivers."[11]

As a near-term event, the exhibition race in Japan has created economic opportunities for the sport, sponsors, and licensees. Kodak, McDonald's, Goodyear, Ford, and Chevrolet are deeply committed to international sales and by showcasing NASCAR in Japan, these companies hope to further tap that market. When Dale Earnhardt drove the race, it was not in his customary black Goodwrench Service Chevrolet. Instead he drove the blue AC Delco car because General Motors wanted to promote its parts division to the Japanese.

The NASCAR Success

If you asked Bill France, Jr., what is the driving force in NASCAR's success, he would tell you it is the "product there on the racetrack— the competition, the color, charisma, the personalities involved."[12]

He is right. The product has made NASCAR Winston Cup racing the fastest growing spectator sport in the country. But to reduce NASCAR's success singularly to the sport overlooks several other contributing factors.

The growth of stock car racing has been rather steady since 1972, the year when RJR Reynolds became the sport's primary sponsor. But the fastest rate of growth has occurred over the past ten years, a period that coincidentally tracks the growth of the corporate world's acceptance of sponsorship as an effective marketing tool. This is not to imply that NASCAR's success is simply the result of being in the right place at the right time. Yes, stock car racing lends itself very well to sponsorship; but what has set NASCAR far ahead of the NFL, NBA, or MLB is how well it has mastered the sponsorship relationship.

If you ask organizational experts what traits are necessary for a company to thrive and succeed, adaptability and flexibility will certainly be on their list. No other sports organization has as much flexibility in its sponsorship programs as does NASCAR. It does not force companies to accept prepackaged programs on a take-it-or-leave-it basis. Instead, it works hard to adapt its sponsorship opportunities to the needs of a sponsoring company.

NASCAR's sponsorship programs, in relative and absolute terms, are also very affordable. All companies—small-town family businesses as well as the Fortune 500—are warmly welcomed as potential NASCAR sponsors. This is not to say that NASCAR's level of marketing sophistication is small-time. Terms like "integrated marketing tool" and "complete marketing package" are central to NASCAR's thinking. Whenever possible, NASCAR does encourage companies to seek out promotional opportunities, advertising support, and media time as complements to their sponsorship. However, when marketing dollars do not allow for extensive campaigns,

NASCAR's good manners would never permit the sport to be ungrateful.

Today, more than 250 companies, including 70 of the Fortune 500, put up over a quarter of a billion dollars for the privilege of sponsoring stock car racing. This sport is not only about beer, tobacco, oil, and gasoline. Megamarketers like the Coca-Cola Company, PepsiCo, Procter & Gamble, and Kodak have found their way to NASCAR for one simple, bottom-line reason: they have learned that their customers are going to stock car races. They have determined that the fans know and appreciate the sponsors. And they know that, more than in any other sport, stock car fans put their money where their loyalty is.

4

PRIME TIME

NEAL PILSON COULD not believe what he was seeing. Instead of the bright sunshine he had confidently expected, all that was visible through the window of the broadcast booth high above Daytona International Speedway was the fierce gray sky and the cold hard rain pelting the racetrack. The winter sun that is Florida's trademark was blocked behind a broad weather front spread across the entire eastern United States, putting the biggest gamble of Pilson's professional life in serious jeopardy.

No one in the booth felt like talking. The only sound was the soft squeak of Pilson's shoes as he paced back and forth in front of the window. Finally, Gene Jankowski, president of CBS Television, voiced what everyone was thinking. "We don't have to pay for this race if it rains, do we?"

Pilson felt his stomach sink. He turned from the window and faced his boss. "We are obligated to pay for the broadcast rights," he said, trying to keep the anxiety from his voice, "despite the rain."[1]

It was February 1979. Pilson, head of business affairs for CBS, and Barry Frank, vice president of CBS Sports, had negotiated the complete live broadcast of the Daytona 500, the first time a network had carried full flag-to-flag coverage of a major race. Until then, with one minor exception (live broadcast of a short, 100-mile race in 1971), television coverage of stock car racing had been limited to tape-delayed excerpts. The idea of setting aside four hours to televise a live race in its entirety was revolutionary. Many in the industry felt it was too risky. Would viewers actually sit still for four hours to watch a stock car race? How would a national audience respond to a sport linked primarily to the South?

CBS had made a significant investment in the Daytona 500. Advertisers had committed several million dollars, part of which would have to be returned if the race was postponed. Production costs were over $400,000, which didn't include the cost of entertaining several broadcast and advertising executives who had come to Daytona to witness the historic event. And the broadcast rights, which had to be paid whether the race ran today or not, had cost $500,000.

The Daytona 500 had never been canceled because of weather. Now, one hour before race time, the atmosphere in the CBS broadcasting booth was somber. Down below, along pit row, each stock car was draped with rain-soaked canvas covers. Fans were huddled underneath jackets, parkas, and makeshift tarps. While the CBS brass were tallying up what this fiasco was going to cost them, Bill France, Jr. popped his head in to say what everyone already knew: the race was going to be delayed.

Then, at eleven-thirty, one half hour before race time, Big Bill France burst through the doors. If he was worried, he didn't show it. In the boisterous way that was his normal style, he greeted everyone in the room, grinning and slapping people on the back, reassuring everyone that of course there would be a race. Then he stepped outside the booth, walked up the steps to the tower roof, and with both arms raised to the sky, *commanded* the rain to cease.

Which it did.

Today, Pilson says no one remembers who noticed it first, but shortly before twelve noon, the rain stopped and the clouds began to clear. Pit crews quickly folded back their canvas covers, drivers headed toward their cars, and fans began to remove their rain gear. Maintenance workers in special pickup trucks steadily circled the track, drying the asphalt. At forty minutes past the hour, just twenty minutes later than scheduled, the Grand Marshal bellowed into the loudspeaker, "Gentlemen, start your engines!" The 1979 Daytona 500 was set to begin.

Ken Squier, the popular CBS announcer, called the race that day, and what a race it was. There were thirty-six lead changes among thirteen different drivers. The caution flag was waved seven times, for fifty-seven laps, in what became an accident-packed race. But nothing prepared the fans or the television viewers for what happened on the backstretch on the last lap of the race.

Cale Yarborough and Donnie Allison, brother of famed stock car driver Bobby Allison, were locked into a dead heat dashing for the checkered flag. The pair, who had scuffled more than once during the race, were now a comfortable twelve seconds ahead of the pack. Barreling down the 3,000-foot backstretch, Yarborough ducked down low in an attempt to pass Allison and race to the finish line. But Allison had other ideas. "Cale had made up his mind he would pass me low," he said, "and I had my mind made up he was going to pass me high."[2] Keeping his car tight up against Yarborough's, Allison forced Yarborough into the infield. Instead of backing off, Yarborough, without lifting the throttle, came roaring back onto the track and hooked Allison. Both cars careened into the third-turn wall and then crashed back into the infield.

CBS had its cameras focused on the two lead drivers, so the entire wreck unfolded on television with Ken Squier yelling, "There's a

wreck on the backstretch! There's a wreck on the backstretch!"
Within seconds, the rest of the pack was coming out of turn two,
heading straight for the crash site.

Richard Petty, the most famous stock car driver in NASCAR, got
word on his radio about the wreck. Petty stood on the pedal and
passed both A. J. Foyt and Darrell Waltrip. As the three drivers
charged past the wreck, CBS cameras picked up the leaders, and
Ken Squier, without missing a beat, called the race home. Richard
Petty held off Darrell Waltrip to win his unprecedented sixth Daytona 500. The fans went crazy: King Richard had done it again.

But the action didn't stop there. Within seconds, Ken Squier
began screaming again. "There's a fight on the backstretch! There's
a fight on the backstretch!" The CBS cameras quickly switched to
the crash site just in time to catch Cale Yarborough brawling with
Bobby Allison, who had stopped his car to check on his brother
Donnie. Fists were swinging wildly as crew men rushed to separate
the two drivers. It was an unbelievable scene, and it was all on live
television. Later that year, CBS won a National Academy of Television Arts and Sciences Emmy award for the telecast.

No one at CBS knew what kind of ratings to expect from the Daytona 500 telecast. Estimates ranged from a low of 2 to an optimistic 5
or 6. (A rating is the size, in percentage terms, of the television audience for a particular show relative to the total sample of TV viewers
in the same time period.) Back in New York, when the returns came
in, CBS executives were stunned. The 1979 Daytona 500 earned an
incredible 10.5 rating; in the last half hour of the race, the rating
went to an even more incredible 13.5. In the same time period, ABC
drew a 9.4 rating for its Superstars competition, and NBC, which
showed a golf tournament, earned a 5.4 rating.

The 10.5 rating meant that 15,000,000 people had watched the
race. There were 125,000 race fans at the track that day, which

was impressive enough, but 15,000,000 television viewers meant that NASCAR had reached millions of new people for the first time. Even the venerable *New York Times* could not ignore the event. "It was like Arnold Palmer winning another Masters. Joe Namath winning another Super Bowl. Willis Reed scoring the game-winning basket," wrote James Tuite.[3] Tuite's detailed and spirited article, which appeared on page one of the sports section, was accompanied by a quarter-page picture of the famous wreck. NASCAR had run its best race while the country watched, and now everyone knew about those fast-driving, hot-tempered, risk-taking stock car drivers.

The day after the Daytona 500, the telephone switchboard lit up at Rockingham's North Carolina Motor Speedway, known to race fans and drivers as The Rock. The next NASCAR race would be held there, and already fans were scrambling for seats. Frank Wilson, vice president of North Carolina Motor Speedway, was all smiles. "The inquiries are coming from all over the country," he said. "They have to be the people who were attracted by what they saw on TV."[4]

Throughout the 1970s, stock car racing had seen strong growth in fan attendance. When the R.J. Reynolds Tobacco Company began sponsoring stock car racing in 1971, the company helped many tracks clean and improve their facilities. The crisp new red and white paint (the colors of Winston cigarettes) that adorned the tracks was courtesy of R.J. Reynolds. The company sent some of its best marketing executives to help local track owners better promote their races. In 1972, NASCAR reduced the number of Winston Cup events to thirty-one. Fewer races were held at better facilities promoted by smarter people, and the number of fans attending a NASCAR race on a per-event basis began to rise.

With improved racetracks and a strong underlying fan base, NASCAR was well positioned to take the next step. But without national television exposure, the sport would be forever shackled within its region. The CBS broadcast of the Daytona 500 brought instant credibility to the sport while formally introducing stock car racing to the rest of the country. It was a momentous event in the history of the sport.

CBS's 1979 Daytona success led to more races and more innovations. In-car cameras, a technology brought over from races in the Australian outback, proved to be a big hit with viewers. At first, drivers wanted nothing to do with in-car cameras. The equipment was large and bulky and considered a distraction by most drivers. Then Cale Yarborough, who had agreed to ride with an onboard camera, won the 1983 Daytona 500. For the first time, viewers could watch a stock car race from the driver's angle. When Yarborough took the checkered flag while pumping his fist in the air, they felt as if they were riding alongside him.

Each time a race was shown on TV, stock car racing witnessed a surge in fan interest. What NASCAR badly needed was a way to show more races. The answer came in the form of cable television. When ESPN, the Entertainment and Sports Programming Network, burst on the scene in the early 1980s, it was hungry for programming. The Big Three networks were already the broadcast home to football, basketball, baseball, golf, tennis, and the Olympics. The one sport that had plenty of inventory and no takers was stock car racing.

In 1980, Steven M. Bornstein, then president of ESPN, began negotiating his network's first auto racing agreements. In 1981, ESPN broadcast its first Winston Cup race, the Carolina 500 at Rockingham. In 1982, the cable network caught Benny Parsons driving the first stock car over 200 miles an hour during a qualifying run at Talladega Superspeedway. ESPN was there again in 1985 when Bill

Elliott earned the first $1 million Winston bonus with a win at Darlington. In 1989, ESPN began telecasting the Pepsi 400, Daytona International Speedway's summer Winston Cup race.

That same year, The Nashville Network (TNN) also began broadcasting Winston Cup races. ESPN, for the first time, was confronted with a hungry competitor that wanted motorsports. TNN had targeted as its primary audience those viewers interested in the southern country lifestyle—in other words, NASCAR's most passionate fans. Instantly, NASCAR Winston Cup races became TNN's highest rated program.

Therein lies one of the two principal reasons why the broadcast rights to NASCAR Winston Cup racing have become so precious: consistently high ratings. The second reason, as we will see, can be traced to the scarcity of the event. There is only one race per week.

The Ratings Game

According to Nielsen Media Research, over 148 million people watched NASCAR Winston Cup racing in 1996. The television ratings for this series have been steadily rising since 1990. CBS reports that its Winston Cup events averaged a 6.1 rating in 1996—20 percent higher than in 1995, and a 22 percent increase since 1990. At ABC, its 1996 Winston Cup ratings averaged a 4.9 rating—an 11 percent increase over 1995, and 23 percent higher than in 1990.

The results from the cable networks have been impressive as well. ESPN reports that its Winston Cup ratings have increased an amazing 50 percent since 1990. In 1996, ESPN averaged a 4.2 rating for its sixteen events, including a record-setting 5.5 rating for its telecast of the Winston Select 500 race at Talladega. ESPN has become accustomed to breaking records by showing NASCAR events.

Its 1996 ratings were 8 percent better than its 3.9 rating in 1995 and 31 percent higher than its 1994 rating. Today, NASCAR Winston Cup racing has become the second highest rated sporting event, after NFL football, on ESPN.

"We saw a big jump in 1995," explains John Wildhack, senior vice president of programming at ESPN, "because of the excitement centering around Jeff Gordon and Dale Earnhardt."[5] Viewers were locked in on Jeff Gordon, NASCAR's fastest-rising star. Gordon, who is young, attractive, and well spoken, battled Dale Earnhardt, the veteran superstar, throughout the season. At twenty-four, Gordon electrified the world of stock car racing by becoming the youngest Winston Cup Champion, edging out Earnhardt by a mere thirty-four points.

NASCAR's ratings success over the past several years is all the more amazing when compared against the rest of the sporting world. While stock car racing has been experiencing rapid growth in ratings, other sports have suffered with ratings decline.[6] In 1996, from September to December, all sporting events were seen by 17 percent fewer households. For professional football, 1996 was a new low. Ratings for the NFL season dropped 5 percent at Fox, ABC, and CBS; cable viewership declined by 10 percent. For baseball, the news was worse. The World Series posted its third lowest rating ever in 1996, and the All-Star Game earned its lowest rating since 1965. Only NBA basketball has been able to keep its viewership, a fact attributed almost singularly to the Michael Jordan effect.

To fully understand television ratings in the sporting business, we must draw a distinction between regular-season events and playoff/championship events. It is perhaps no surprise that the Super Bowl and the NFL's divisional playoffs remain the highest-rated sporting events; NFL football, despite its ratings decline over the past several years, is still the highest rated sport. The NBA championship series averages a 14 rating, and the World Series averages an impressive 19. By comparison, stock car racing drops to fourth place.

However, if we compare NASCAR's Winston Cup series to the *regular-season* games of football, baseball, and basketball, we discover something interesting. Over the five-year period from 1992 to 1996, Winston Cup races averaged a 5.6 rating—higher than NBA games (4.6) or Major League Baseball (3.9). Only professional football does better: a 12 rating for CBS and Fox games, a 17 for Monday Night Football, ABC's prime-time telecast. So, during the other sports' regular season, NASCAR racing is the second highest rated sporting event.

The reason NASCAR events do so well all season long is the same reason the other sports do so well during the playoffs: the thrill of seeing the sport's best athletes compete in a one-time event. By the time baseball, basketball, and football get to the playoffs, the very best teams are facing each other. Each game in a playoff series takes on an intensity that increases geometrically; as the stakes rise, so does the excitement. So too does the sense of urgency. Fans know that playoff and championship games will be played only once, and they had better not miss them.

NASCAR does not have a championship event. What it has instead is a limited number of equally weighted races in which, by virtue of qualifying runs that eliminate the merely great, only the very best athletes compete. That limited schedule is a key reason why Winston Cup racing generates such high television ratings.

"Winston Cup racing," explains Neal Pilson, "is appointment television." There is only one Winston Cup race each weekend. At this race, the top drivers come together to race against each other. If you're a fan, there is only one chance each week to catch a race. Now compare this to football, basketball, or baseball. On any given weekend, there could be several games to choose from, not counting at least one more during the week. Miss one game, and you can easily catch another within a day or so.

Since the mid-1980s, it has become harder to sell sports to consumers because of the proliferation of product. With so much to choose from, and so many different times to watch a chosen sport, the value of each event has begun to decline. NASCAR's value, on the other hand, is found in its limited supply. This is reflected not only in its ratings, but in the dollar value of its broadcast rights— the fees that networks pay for the privilege of broadcasting an event.

More and more, the business of televising football, basketball, and baseball has become the quintessential loss leader. The advertising revenue generated during the regular season doesn't cover the billions of dollars paid for these broadcast rights. The big money is made at the season's end when championship games are televised and advertisers are willing to pay top dollar in exchange for larger audiences.

NASCAR is a different story.

Billions for Broadcast Rights

Interestingly, ratings, while important, are not central for determining rights fees. Ratings are important to advertisers, who seek to reach the greatest number of people. "However, rights fees are determined differently," explains Pilson, who now heads a consulting firm that negotiates broadcast rights. "Broadcast competition really determines rights fees," he points out, "and so long as there is a shortage of events there will always be high demand for rights fees."

Imagine if you went to an airline ticket counter to purchase a ticket and found there were three passengers, including yourself, vying for one open seat. With several interested parties, the value of the seat might rise far above its cost. Such is the formula for determining the broadcast rights for NASCAR races. Today, there are three interested parties vying for NASCAR events: ABC/ESPN, CBS/TNN, and Time Warner/TBS; a fourth—the Fox network—is expressing interest. Already it is clear that the cost of broadcast rights is on the rise.

Who Owns the Broadcast Rights?

At the National Football League, National Basketball Association, and Major League Baseball, the organizations negotiate broadcast rights on behalf of the clubs. When a contract is agreed on, the dollar amount is divided equally among the clubs. In stock car racing, broadcast rights are negotiated differently. NASCAR does not own the rights to Winston Cup events nor does it negotiate TV rights. Instead, each track owns its rights and negotiates those rights individually. NASCAR receives 10 percent of the total broadcast fee.

When CBS approached Bill France, Jr. to broadcast the 1979 Daytona 500, the network did not negotiate with NASCAR but rather with International Speedway Corporation, the company that owns Daytona International Speedway. At that time, CBS paid International Speedway $1.5 million for the right to broadcast the Daytona 500 in three successive years.

Until 1996, broadcast rights for many Winston Cup races were less than $1 million. Daytona was in a class by itself, charging CBS $4.2 million for the rights to broadcast its race. But the day when you could broadcast a NASCAR Winston Cup race for less than $1 million is over. "NASCAR has done a tremendous job marketing this sport," points out Rudy Martzke, a reporter who writes the "Sports on TV" column for *USA Today*. "I don't see any reason why broadcast rights can't go higher."[7] And higher is definitely where they are heading. The broadcast rights for the 1997 inaugural races at Texas Motor Speedway and California Speedway cost more than $3 million, and for the Daytona 500 weekend, including the Saturday support race, rights doubled to $8.5 million.

Broadcast rights are not the only cost facing networks. In 1979, the production cost of the Daytona 500 was approximately $400,000. At the 1997 Daytona 500, CBS put seventy cameras to work at a cost somewhere between $1.5 and $2 million. Today, in addition to several cameras positioned high above the track, there are cameras inches from the track, remote cameras along pit row, and tiny remote cameras inside many race cars.

Thankfully for the networks, as production costs and broadcast rights have risen, so too has the value of advertising times. You could telecast a thirty-second commercial at the 1979 Daytona 500 for between $25,000 and $30,000. Today, a thirty-second commercial for the Daytona 500 costs over $130,000. For NASCAR events, says ESPN's John Wildhack, "We are seeing significant demand for advertising."

There is nothing on the horizon to suggest that the competition for NASCAR broadcast rights—and hence the value for those rights—is declining. Already, CBS and ABC are staking out competitive positions. "Our relationship with ISC [International Speedway Corporation], Bill France, and NASCAR is one of our oldest and most valued," said Steven M. Bornstein, ESPN president and now CEO/president of ABC Sports. "It is the core of our year-round dedication to motorsports. We are pleased to remain the race fan's primary source of Winston Cup racing."[8] ESPN has backed those words with action. During the 1997 racing season, ESPN broadcast eighteen of the thirty-two Winston Cup events.

But CBS Television will not be outdone. "There is no more exciting sport from all angles than NASCAR racing," claims Sean

McManus, president of CBS Sports. "The ratings and sales continue to climb, the national interest is greater every year, and the innovative production opportunities make this programming as compelling as anything on television."[9]

CBS's infatuation with NASCAR has grown over the years. The Daytona 500 has always ranked as one of the network's highest-rated sporting events. But recently, the Daytona 500 has begun to outperform the NBA playoffs, the NHL Stanley Cup Finals, and the Kentucky Derby. Just as important, NASCAR on CBS became the leading sport among the advertisers' most cherished demographic: males aged eighteen to forty-nine and twenty-five to fifty-four. The demographics were stronger than college football, PGA golf, and the U.S. Open tennis championships.

In early 1997, McManus predicted that CBS would "play a crucial role in NASCAR's future growth." The words were prophetic. Within weeks, Westinghouse/CBS announced the $1.55 billion acquisition of Gaylord Entertainment's two cable networks, Country Music Television (CMT) and The Nashville Network (TNN), both of them rich with NASCAR fans.

TNN has become the franchise for country lifestyles: country music performances and talk shows, bass fishing, hunting, and motorsports—including the broadcast rights to seven Winston Cup events. The acquisition gave CBS/TNN control of eleven of NASCAR's thirty-two Winston Cup race dates. In addition, CBS acquired another important piece of the NASCAR mosaic: NASCAR Thunder, a chain of licensed NASCAR-themed retail stores.

According to Michael Jordan, chairman and chief executive of Westinghouse/CBS, the acquisition of TNN and CMT "was a strategic move to expand the reach and scope of CBS's media businesses into high growth segments." With the acquisition, CBS was now a powerhouse in the country music and country lifestyle franchise. "The opportunity," explained Jordan, "allows CBS to develop programming jointly for broadcast and cable, and to cross-promote all our media properties."[10] In one bold stroke, Jordan has been able to position CBS/TNN in much the same way ABC leverages its position with ESPN.

NASCAR Programming Extensions

The ESPN and TNN telecast schedules are loaded with racing programs. On weekends, TNN broadcasts "Raceday," a motorsports roundup program with a heavy emphasis on NASCAR racing series. TNN also broadcasts two other NASCAR programs. "Inside NASCAR" is owned by TNN, licensed by NASCAR, and produced by Sun Belt Video for the benefit of TNN's viewers. "NASCAR Garage" is produced by Ross Television and shown on TNN in a cooperative arrangement with NASCAR in order to promote its new auto after-market licensing group.

ESPN counters with "Speedweek," a motorsports program equivalent to TNN's "Raceday." But ABC's greatest contribution to NASCAR racing is found in its new brand extension—ESPN2. Known as "the deuce," ESPN2 has greatly expanded ABC's ability to showcase NASCAR and Winston Cup racing. Each weekend, the deuce telecasts RPM 2Day, a motorsports information program; seven days a week, it offers RPM 2Night, a nightly update on motorsports.

ESPN2 also gives ABC the opportunity to broadcast more Winston Cup action by televising qualifying trials and the practice sessions referred to as "happy hour." Typically, following a Busch Grand National race on Saturday, happy hour is reserved for Winston Cup drivers to practice one last time before Sunday's race.

In all, not a day goes by when you can't get some programming on racing specific to NASCAR. Both ESPN and TNN now televise live all Busch Grand National races as well as NASCAR's Craftsman Truck series. During the week, both cable networks replay qualifying runs, practice sessions, and the races from the previous weekend: Winston Cup, Busch Grand National, and Craftsman Truck races.

Throughout the racing season, ESPN, TNN, and TBS telecast NASCAR specials. ESPN, for example, has televised "The Glory Days: Darlington 1966" and "The Glory Days: Junior Johnson." TNN has broadcast specials such as "The Darrell Waltrip Story." In short, there appears to be no shortage of programming opportunities in NASCAR. The reason networks are filling their time slots with racing is quite simple: because fans are watching.

Lastly, the symbiotic relationship between the two network/cable pairs (ABC/ESPN and CBS/TNN) allows them to cross promote programs. ESPN's RPM 2Day, on the air immediately before a Winston Cup race on ABC, will hand-deliver viewers to the ABC time slot. ESPN2, during its broadcasts of qualifying and practice sessions for the Winston Cup race, constantly reminds viewers the race will be shown on ABC Sunday afternoon. Broadcast rights, programming specials, flexibility, and cross promotion afford ABC/ESPN and CBS/TNN the opportunity to exploit NASCAR's popularity.

Broadcast Rights Take a Big Jump

If Neal Pilson and Rudy Martzke were correct in their bullish assumptions about NASCAR, the evidence should be apparent each time broadcast rights are renegotiated. We didn't have to wait long to see that evidence.

International Speedway Corporation, which owns the famous tracks at Daytona, Darlington, Talladega, and Watkins Glen, was set, in 1997, to negotiate a long-term deal for the broadcast rights to its races. Both ESPN and CBS, as we might imagine, were intensely interested, and when the negotiations were completed both networks came away with a prize.

ESPN locked up a four-year deal (1998–2001) to broadcast eleven events, including two NASCAR Winston Cup races each at Darlington and Talladega, and a fifth Winston Cup race at Watkins Glen. In addition, there were four NASCAR Busch Grand National races (two at Darlington, one at Talladega, one at Watkins Glen), a Busch North series race in Watkins Glen, and an ARCA-sanctioned race at Talladega (the Automobile Racing Club of America is a stock car sanctioning body similar to, but far smaller than, NASCAR). The price tag: a reported $55 million.

CBS kept the Daytona package. For the same four-year period (1998–2001), CBS bought the rights to broadcast the Daytona 500 (the most popular race) and the Pepsi 400, the summer Winston Cup race also held at Daytona. In addition, CBS will broadcast two Daytona Busch Grand National races, the Busch Clash (an all-star race of previous Busch pole winners), the Daytona Busch pole qualifying, and the twin Gatorade 125s, an additional qualifying requirement for the Daytona 500. The cost: a reported $80 million. Another $8 million for NASCAR.

All told, the four-year deal negotiated by International Speedway Corporation set the value for its races over the next four years at $135 million—a far cry from the days when networks, with the exception of the Daytona 500, could broadcast races for a few hundred thousand dollars. Even so, both networks appear happy. They have a long-term deal to televise America's fastest-growing sport. "If more sports had competitors, team owners, and organizers like

NASCAR," CBS's McManus comments, "the sports world would be a much more pleasant place to make one's living."[11]

Radio Holds Its Own

Long before television began broadcasting NASCAR events, it was still possible for stock car fans to catch a race even if they couldn't make it to the track. Radio has played an important role in all major sports, but its role in NASCAR has particular meaning. In the 1950s, 1960s, and 1970s, fans of baseball, football, and basketball turned on the television to watch their weekly games. But stock car fans, because NASCAR came late to television broadcasting, had no choice but to listen to their sport on radio. You couldn't always see Junior Johnson, Richard Petty, or Bobby Allison charge around the track, but with a radio nearby you could always hear the excitement.

When network television began to broadcast stock car races, many radio listeners turned to their television sets. That was to be expected. Stock car racing is a colorful sport full of fast-paced action, and television provides a visual dimension that radio cannot. But to dismiss radio broadcasts of stock car races as no longer relevant overlooks the inherent value of radio itself.

Even though television dominates in sheer numbers, radio has carved out an important niche for consumers. That niche is portability and convenience. An on-the-go society, we turn to radio for entertainment and information while driving in the car, working outdoors, or sitting on the beach. And, in an interesting twist, many of the 150,000 fans who attend a race also listen to the radio broadcast on their headsets. There may be upward of 5 million people watching Winston Cup racing on television each Sunday, but there are 2.5 million more listening to the race on radio.

Today, radio coverage of NASCAR races is produced primarily by the Motor Racing Network (MRN), an independent operating subsidiary of International Speedway Corporation. Each season, MRN packages forty events (twenty-nine Winston Cup races and eleven Busch Grand National races) and broadcasts them to 450 radio affiliates covering approximately 83 percent of the country.

The package costs a radio station $2,000 for the season. This might not sound like a lot of money, but in fact it is noteworthy that the station pays anything at all; in a typical network/affiliate relationship, the network often pays the affiliate to carry the program. For MRN, the $2,000 fee from each affiliate helps to offset the production expenses and the cost of renting four hours of satellite time on SAT Com C-5.

To make a profit, radio affiliates sell advertising time for each race. A four-hour Winston Cup race, for example, affords a station twenty-four minutes of advertising time. The price the station can charge for advertising depends on the size of the market and the station's ranking within the market. On average, a middle-ranked radio station in a smaller market might charge approximately $50 for a thirty-second spot. Each Winston Cup race would generate about $2,400 advertising revenue for the station, or $69,000 for all twenty-nine Winston Cup races.

Top-ranked radio stations in larger markets are able to charge much higher ad rates. For example, at WGST-AM in Atlanta and WFOC-FM in Charlotte, two very popular radio stations, one thirty-second commercial costs approximately $130. These stations take in about $6,200 per event, or $180,000 for twenty-nine Winston Cup races. For this amount of revenue, paying $2,000 to MRN for a season of stock car racing is a profitable investment indeed.

"Unquestionably it has been profitable for me," reports Wayne Harris, station manager and owner of WNPC-FM in Newport,

Tennessee.[12] For years, WNPC had broadcast the University of Tennessee football games. Then Harris, while driving across North Carolina one day, happened to dial in a NASCAR race. He was so taken with the broadcast, he decided to make a switch. "Stock car racing had an immediate impact on our advertising sales," Harris remembers, "and we have been growing steadily ever since. Now our biggest problem is not who you are going to sell advertising to, it's who you are going to turn down."

Radio broadcasts of NASCAR races have always been popular in the South, but lately MRN has convinced many northern radio stations to broadcast NASCAR Winston Cup racing as well. "I was pretty skeptical going in," admits Dale Jones, programming director at WZBG-FM in Litchfield, Connecticut.[13] "After all, we are an adult contemporary music radio station." But it didn't take long before Jones knew he had made the right decision. "I am convinced now," he says, "because our listeners and advertisers have responded so well."

The rising economics of NASCAR racing are being felt by radio stations all across the country. Southern stations and northern, large markets and small—all are profiting from the growing interest in stock car racing. "Bottom line," explains Chris Wallace, general manager at WDSD-FM in Dover, Delaware, "broadcasting NASCAR races makes a lot of money for us."[14]

Wallace estimates that about 25 percent of the station's weekly audience tunes in on Sunday afternoon between 12:00 and 4:00 to catch the race. The demand for advertising is centered around this time period as well. "We sell three quarters of our advertising inventory before the NASCAR season starts," Wallace says. "We hold back a quarter of our inventory for those who we know will catch the racing fever."

Like the affiliate stations, MRN itself has also been able to profit from advertiser interest in NASCAR. Each four-hour Winston Cup race produces a total of forty-eight minutes of advertising time. The affiliates are allowed to sell twenty-four minutes to local advertisers, and MRN keeps the other twenty-four, to sell to national advertisers. Who purchases these ad spots? Many of the same companies that sponsor events or race teams. Radio helps these companies cross promote and enhance their sponsorship image within NASCAR.

How profitable is this national advertising? In 1980, an advertiser could get a sixty-second network radio spot on MRN for about $1,000. Today, that same sixty seconds costs over $6,000.

Newspapers and Racing Publications

Considering the origins of stock car racing, it is not surprising that the first reporters to cover the sport worked for southern newspapers. Many of these sports writers covered all local events: college football, basketball, and an occasional farm-team baseball game. As stock car racing grew in popularity, these same reporters were asked to pick up an additional assignment.

"I can't believe the growth," muses long-time reporter Tom Higgins.[15] "When I started to cover the sport, the grandstands were wooden, the restrooms were military latrines out in the woods, and most tracks were dirt and dusty." Higgins is a qualified historian. He has seen more stock car racing than any other newspaper reporter. Higgins began covering NASCAR for the *Asheville (N.C.) Citizen Times* in 1957. Then, in 1964, he moved to the *Charlotte Observer* to cover stock car racing, where he stayed until his retirement in 1996. He now writes a column for *NASCAR Winston Cup Scene*, a weekly paper that covers Winston Cup, Busch Grand National, and the Craftsman Truck series.

"Atlantic Coast Conference basketball has always been big in North Carolina," explained Higgins. "However, in the late 1970s, the paper ran a survey and was surprised to learn that stock car racing's popularity among readers was second, by a slim margin, to ACC basketball." Based on that survey, Higgins recalls, the paper dramatically increased its linage for stock car racing.

The story was the same with many other southern newspapers. Soon, NASCAR coverage shared front-page space with the popular college sports. But it would be years before NASCAR would break through its regional barriers. For almost forty-five years, NASCAR was all but ignored by northern newspapers and magazines. The *New York Times* sent a reporter to each Daytona 500, but often that was the only race covered by the paper for the entire season.

With the sport's growing popularity, newspapers and magazines have begun to increase their coverage of NASCAR events. However, the real breakthrough for NASCAR came in 1995, when *USA Today* dramatically altered its coverage of the sport—an editorial change that was very slow in coming. Steve Ballard, motorsports editor at *USA Today* for the past eight years, remembers the painful struggles to get more coverage for NASCAR. "For the first five years I was at the paper, I wanted to quit," he recalled. "Each day, I had to fight other reporters and editors for space. It was a losing proposition. Football, basketball, and baseball stories were always given preferential treatment."[16]

Then, in 1995, the paper suddenly changed. The break for NASCAR, Ballard recalls, came when *USA Today* started to compare demographics. John Griffin, director of communications for NASCAR, remembers the same thing.

Griffin and other NASCAR executives had arranged a meeting with the editors of *USA Today*, to present NASCAR and the sport of stock car racing in hopes of encouraging more editorial coverage. The evening before the presentation, the NASCAR group had gathered for an informal meeting. "Someone had a demographic report of the paper's readers," Griffin recalls.[17] "The meeting went quiet. "We all stared in disbelief. Their numbers were our numbers!"

What Griffin saw in the report was that the demographic profile of a USA Today reader was exactly like the demographic profile of a NASCAR fan. "We were working with a big misperception," said Ballard. "In fact, NASCAR's demographics parallel our own."

Armed with this knowledge, USA Today aggressively expanded its coverage of NASCAR events. Instead of just a Monday wrapup of the prior weekend's races, the paper began running stories on Fridays. Then NASCAR events began to appear almost daily. Now USA Today, in addition to its daily sports coverage, publishes a special Thursday motorsports edition that is largely dedicated to NASCAR racing.

"Personally, it's been very gratifying," Ballard confesses. "There is now dedicated space in the paper for our stories. My travel budget has been doubled and we are now attending every NASCAR Winston Cup event. As far as USA Today is concerned, the paper acknowledges NASCAR's importance in the sporting world."

Sports Illustrated got a wake-up call a few years ago as well. In July 1995, Michael Silver's piece on NASCAR, "A Day at the Races," was the magazine's cover story. It was the second best selling newsstand issue that year, second only to the enormously popular swimsuit edition.

It is important to remember that Sports Illustrated is the perennial "stick and ball" sports magazine. It is 93 percent subscriber based, with only a few hundred thousand copies sold on newsstands each week. Even so, the surprising popularity of the NASCAR story in 1995 served to realign thinking at the magazine.

Each year, the magazine publishes several special editions, called "*Sports Illustrated* Presents," dedicated to individual sports: college football and basketball; professional football, basketball, and baseball. In 1997, for the first time, there was a special edition on NASCAR: "*Sports Illustrated* Presents 1996 Winston Cup—A Season to Remember." The results were remarkable.

"The edition sold extraordinarily well," reports Dave Mingy, public relations executive for the magazine; "way above expectations, with sales comparable to our other 'SI Presents' editions. In addition, the ad rates for this category were well above what we projected."[18]

Stephen Madden, editor for the "SI Presents" series, was equally gratified. "There was a time at *Sports Illustrated* when editors weren't comfortable calling themselves motorsports editors," he recalls.[19] "Sure, we attended the Daytona 500 and the Indy 500 but not much else." But *Sports Illustrated* was looking for ways to expand its base, and the success of the NASCAR issues could not be ignored. When magazine staffers compared the demographics of NASCAR fans to the demographics of its own readers, Madden remembers thinking, "We are these people." It was almost exactly the same experience as at *USA Today*, and with very similar results: greatly increased coverage of NASCAR and stock car racing.

Special Publications

Stock car racing, just like other sports, boasts several specialty magazines and newspapers that cover the sport exclusively. *NASCAR Winston Cup Scene*, a weekly newspaper published since 1977, counts 1.5 million readers. It is owned by Street & Smith Publications, which also owns *NASCAR Winston Cup Illustrated*, a monthly magazine published since 1983. General Media Automotive Group publishes *Stock Car Racing*, also a monthly magazine.

Two newer magazines covering the sport have come onto the scene. *Racing for Kids*, owned jointly by Dale Earnhardt and Jeff Gordon, is published monthly by Championship Publishing. *Inside NASCAR* is a relatively new publication from the Quarton Group, a company that also publishes *NBA's Inside Stuff* and *NHL Powerplay Magazine*. A quarterly magazine, *Inside NASCAR* focuses on the "people" side of the sport. In all, there are twelve licensed publications that publish information on NASCAR, including the programs for all Winston Cup races.

What does expanded newspaper coverage mean for NASCAR? What does the advent of specialty magazines mean for the sport? On a very obvious level, expanded coverage is a testament to the sport's enlarged fan base. But NASCAR argues, with justification, that fan attendance has always warranted this amount of print coverage. So what has changed? It appears that the change has much to do with a conscious shift in editorial direction. Publishing executives, newspaper editors, and reporters are beginning to realize that NASCAR's fans are, and always have been, their readers. To strengthen their subscription base, as well as to attract new readers, newspapers and magazines can no longer afford to ignore our country's fastest-growing sport with its legion of passionate fans.

Televising the Action Sport

Television, radio, and print media have all played an important role in NASCAR's growth over the past fifty years, and each will continue to participate, meaningfully, as the sport moves forward. But the greatest growth opportunity for NASCAR still remains in television. It is the medium that reaches the greatest number of people, and it is the business model that provides the greatest economic potential for the sport.

The bottom line is that NASCAR racing, relative to other national sports programming, remains a cheap buy. NASCAR's broadcasting rights are still demonstrably less than those for football, baseball, and basketball. Yet NASCAR remains the only national sport still capable of increasing its television ratings year after year. As we have seen, television and cable broadcasters, as well as their advertisers, happily acknowledge that NASCAR generates high economic returns for their investment.

For its part, NASCAR is also investing in its television future. Drivers, team owners, and crew chiefs have worked hard to improve their on-camera skills. Dale Earnhardt, after countless commercials, is at ease pitching Burger King in front of a camera. Terry Labonte, holding a bowl of Kellogg's Corn Flakes, looks like a pro. Jeff Gordon, already a superstar on the track, is a superb media performer. Whether appearing with David Letterman on "The Late Show" or standing with his teammates peddling Quaker State Motor Oil, Gordon is a natural. Even Robert Yates, the venerable owner of Robert Yates Racing, does a great job in Texaco's commercials.

In many ways, NASCAR has helped television expand its technological prowess. Broadcasting a stock car race is not a simple undertaking. Not only is the playing field large but the players are moving extremely fast. This combination requires broadcasters to send their very best technicians, cameramen, and directors to cover a race.

The CBS broadcast of the 1997 Daytona 500, for instance, used eighty-seven television cameras, the largest number in motorsports history. In addition to the cameras placed high above the racetrack and at every turn, there were in-ground cameras that captured stock cars at speeds never seen before on television. Cameras attached to jibs hung above pit row so that viewers could have a closeup view of those unbelievable twenty-second pit stops. The 1997 race also introduced the new Akela camera, which provided some of the most amazing views of the race. The camera shot began in the infield, picked up the cars as they came down the frontstretch, then swept out onto the track to catch the blistering speed as the stock cars dove into turn one.

The television techno-wizards assigned to broadcast a stock car race are constantly seeking new ways to televise the action. The 1997 Daytona 500 used ten in-car cameras, a record. Every imaginable angle was used to capture the drama of driving a stock car at 190 miles per hour. There were cameras on the dashboard, focused directly at the driver's face; cameras on the floor to capture the driver's footwork; cameras behind the driver to watch the shifting and maneuvering; cameras underneath the cars to catch the pounding; cameras atop the cars to catch the action up front as well as the cars trailing behind. It seemed that no angle in the race was left to the imagination.

Telephoto lenses, slow motion, and instant replay have taken the broadcasts of stick-and-ball sports as far as they can go, but stock car racing provides many more technical opportunities. Twenty years after the first televised broadcast of the Daytona 500, technicians are still dreaming of ways to televise the action of NASCAR racing.

Even with all its startling camera angles and close-up views, television still cannot completely translate the intensity and excitement of a stock car race. There is simply no substitute for the real thing. You need not become a die-hard fan and attend every race to appreciate stock car racing, but you have to go at least once, for you will never fully enjoy the entertainment of NASCAR racing until you have stood in the stands and felt the thunder.

5

THE MEANEST MILE

HAROLD BRASINGTON WASN'T bothered by the whispers and finger pointing. And that was fortunate, because there were plenty of both that summer of '49. It seemed that no matter where you were—at the grocery store, down at the bank, or at church on Sunday mornings—everyone in Darlington, South Carolina, was talking about Harold and his cockeyed dream. As Jim Hunter, current president of Darlington Raceway, has recorded in his history of the track, the whole town was having one big laugh at Brasington's expense: "Hot-a-mitey, Harold, you gotta be kiddin'! A racetrack for stock cars! That's the craziest thing I ever heard!"[1]

Had Harold planned on building just another dirt track, like the dozens of tracks already sprinkled throughout the Southeast, probably nobody would have paid much attention. But Harold wasn't satisfied with building just another dirt track. His dream was bigger: a 1.25-mile paved speedway so his hometown could host the first ever 500-mile race for stock cars. He planned to build the South's own version of the Indianapolis 500.

Harold Brasington loved racing. He spent most of his free time in the late 1940s traveling around the South to watch stock car races. Back then, the tracks were quarter-mile dirt bowls but the action was still fast and furious, with cars banging into one another until the best took the checkered flag. Then, in 1949, Harold took a quick detour and headed north to Indianapolis to watch the world-famous Indy 500. That trip changed his life.

"I saw all those people up there in Indianapolis and all that excitement. I just figured a big track in Darlington would be the same thing," Brasington recalled. "I got to thinking why a track couldn't be built to run a 500-mile race for stock cars."[2]

It was a bold piece of thinking and, like all daring ideas, not easy to pull off. Fortunately, Harold had some key advantages. First, he was thick-skinned, which helped him overcome the skepticism and the jokes. Second, he was a hell of a salesman. It proved to be the winning combination.

Everywhere he went, Harold tried to sell stock in his racetrack. It didn't matter who you were or where he ran into you, Harold pitched his dream. Harold King, Darlington Raceway's elder statesman, remembers Brasington stopping people on the street and asking if they wanted to buy stock. Most people said the whole idea was silly, King recalls, but "an awful lot of people bought stock and most of them were among those saying how crazy it was."[3]

Barney Wallace, who owned a grocery store near town, allowed himself to be convinced. "A friend of mine worked at the savings and loan," Wallace remembered, "and asked me what I was drawing the money out for. I told him I'm investing in Harold's racetrack."[4] Everyone told Wallace he was crazy and the whole idea of a racetrack was foolishness. But Harold, Wallace recalled, was hard to resist.

Brasington also had one additional advantage. He owned an equipment business and he knew how to operate big machinery. He had convinced Sherman Ramsey, a local plywood salesman, to exchange seventy acres of relatively worthless land outside town for stock in the raceway, and, in December 1949, Harold Brasington set about building his racetrack. Ramsey had put one condition on his deal with Harold: Don't mess with my minnow pond. To avoid the pond, the shape of the track was tightened at one end, creating an egg-shaped oval with a very sharp turn one and turn two that were to bedevil drivers ever after.

Harold was a hardworking man. He used every bit of God's sunshine; when he wasn't moving dirt and rock, he was setting fence posts and building the grandstand. People driving up and down SC Highway 34 would slow down and watch Harold work on his track. "Riding by there then, you'd see where he was piling dirt up for the turns," recalls Margaret Severance, a Darlington native. "You'd pass by again, maybe a few days later, and the dirt would be stacked all up and there Harold would be, no hat and no shirt, sun-burned and dripping with sweat, working like all gid'all!"[5]

Harold was determined to have the track ready for its inaugural race on Labor Day 1950; he intended to call it "The Southern 500." He knew that he would need a sanctioning body not only to run the race but to attract good drivers, so he approached Central States Racing Association (CSRA), which agreed to sanction the race. Soon, however, it was evident that CSRA was having trouble attracting a field. Harold quickly turned to Big Bill France, the tall lanky fellow from Daytona Beach who was having some success in his second year sanctioning races in North Carolina with the National Association of Stock Car Auto Racing. "I told them I really didn't think a track in a little town like Darlington would go," France later told Hunter. "But I agreed to go down and take a look."[6]

Darlington Raceway was still in its early stages, but France could clearly see the outline of Harold's dream. Not only did Big Bill agree to sanction the race, he also agreed to stick around for a few weeks to help Harold with the finishing touches. Now, when people drove by the track, they could see Harold and Big Bill France walking the property, talking about the track and the upcoming race.

By the spring of 1950, Darlington Raceway was beginning to take shape. During the summer, the track was paved and the work on the grandstand was winding down. When finished, it would seat 9,000 spectators. It wasn't long before Darlington's whispers turned into stares of wonder.

It took Big Bill France fifteen days to qualify the field of seventy-five cars for the first Southern 500. While France stayed at the track overseeing the qualifying runs, Harold was out selling tickets. As hard as he worked building the track, Harold worked even harder selling tickets. His concrete bleachers would hold 9,000, but in his own mind, the best Harold expected was 5,000 paying customers.

By Labor Day, Darlington Raceway was ready to host its first event.

The morning of the race, the weather was typical for South Carolina in September—clear and hot. Harold stood in the quiet of the early Monday morning, looking out at his track and wondering what this day would bring.

"We figured we'd make it to the race in plenty of time," remembers Frankie Patterson, then sports editor of *The Kannapolis* (NC) *Independent*. Patterson and a group of friends had left Charlotte early that morning for what they thought would be an easy two-hour drive to the track. "Once we got about 20 miles from Darlington, traffic was bumper-to-bumper, barely creeping along." Patterson figured all these cars must be heading to Myrtle Beach, on the other side of Darlington, until someone commonsensically figured out that by Labor Day Monday, everyone who was going to the beach was already there. "When we finally got to the racetrack, you just wouldn't believe all the people. It was the biggest crowd of people I'd ever seen."[7]

Harold was hoping against hope he could fill the grandstand's 9,000 seats. Absolutely no one imagined that 25,000 people would converge on Darlington that Monday morning. It quickly became apparent that the grandstand would hold only a fraction of the crowd now waiting to get into the track. In desperation, track officials began selling tickets to the infield area. "People were selling tickets and the money was just piled up in the middle of the table," remembers Clarice Lane, who worked in the raceway office that day. "People were running around asking this question and that, and creditors were asking for their money. It was the biggest mess you've ever seen."[8]

Despite the confusion, the first Southern 500 was a big success. Johnny Mantz, driving a 1950 Plymouth, won the race with an average speed of 76 miles per hour and a conservative strategy: he completed the 500 miles without having to change a tire. In those days before hydraulic jacks and air guns, pit stops took minutes, not seconds, to complete. Drivers would often get out of their cars, drink a soda, and eat a hot dog while the crew worked feverishly to change the tires. Mantz knew that driving too fast on asphalt would wear out tires, so while the other drivers barreled around the track at eighty miles an hour, Mantz drove a slower but steady race, gradually picking up position as he passed quicker cars sidelined with blown tires.

After the race, it took hours to empty the infield. The thousands of race fans who had caused the morning traffic jam were now hung up in an evening standstill. It was well after dark, but nobody was complaining. "There wasn't any electricity in the press box," remembers Patterson. Someone found an extension cord and ran it up into the press box, where the newspaper reporters wrote by the light of a single bulb. "The race was great, though," said Patterson, "and none of the guys even thought about typing in the dark. But we were wondering when all those people would get out of the infield; and if they did, would they ever come back for another Southern 500."[9]

With each passing season, Darlington's reputation and attendance grew. In 1952, Fonty Flock, the famed moonshiner from Georgia, won the Southern 500. At victory lane, Fonty, wearing his customary Bermuda shorts, jumped up on the hood of his Oldsmobile 88 and led the crowd of 32,400 in a rendition of "Dixie."

By 1955, the Southern 500 had become the biggest sporting event in the South. Days before the race, all 50,000 tickets had been sold; when the checkered flag dropped on Sunday, the line of cars leading into Darlington was still ten miles long. In 1958, the count was up to 75,000 fans—the expanded track's maximum—and it has stayed there ever since. Year after year, for almost fifty years now, thousands of race fans have trekked to the famous Darlington Raceway. Harold Brasington's dream had come true.

Beyond Darlington

The 1950 Southern 500 had an immediate impact on stock car racing. Track owners began thinking: If a little town like Darlington, South Carolina, could attract 25,000 people, maybe we should take a hard look at our own tracks. A few owners decided to pave their tracks; almost all began adding more seats. Even so, changing NASCAR's "dirt track" image was a slow process. Between 1949 and 1958, 80 percent of NASCAR's events were still held on dirt tracks that were a mile, or less, in length.[10]

There were two attempts, in the early 1950s, to replicate Darlington's success, but, surprisingly, both failed. Raleigh Speedway, a

1-mile paved track, conducted races for only five years (1953–1958) before it closed. The Memphis–Arkansas Speedway, a 1.5-mile banked dirt track, lasted only three years (1954–1957). Many track owners saw this as proof that NASCAR was better suited to short tracks. "The dirt tracks were the backbone of the sport," the traditionalists argued, "and stock car racing would wilt and collapse without the spinal cord intact."[11] But there was someone else who disagreed, and he was as much an idealist as Harold Brasington.

Daytona

Big Bill France had a vision for NASCAR. Its future, he believed, was with tracks like Darlington, not the outdated dirt tracks that still dominated the circuit. He admitted that dirt tracks were still an important part of NASCAR's heritage, and he saluted those track owners who upgraded their facilities. But it was clear to him that the movement toward big tracks was critical for NASCAR's survival. Big Bill wanted to create modern facilities where the racing was more exciting and also where families would feel comfortable. He felt so strongly about this kind of facility that Big Bill risked his entire fortune to build one: Daytona International Speedway.

Although Darlington Raceway is credited with being NASCAR's first superspeedway, world-famous Daytona is the track most responsible for launching the sport of stock car racing into the modern era. Ask any driver his reaction on seeing Daytona for the first time and you will hear words like "amazing," "incredible," and "intimidating." Lee Petty, the father of Richard Petty and winner of the first Daytona 500, remembers the first time he and the other racers drove the track. "I'll tell you what, there wasn't a man there who wasn't scared . . . of the place. We never had raced on a track like that before. Darlington is big, but it wasn't banked like Daytona."[12]

Without question, Daytona was built for speed. It's 2.5 miles long, with big sweeping turns banked at 31 degrees. Fireball Roberts, another famous 1960s NASCAR driver, was eager. "This is the track where you can step on the accelerator and let it roll. You can flatfoot it all the way."[13] And Jimmy Thompson, another driver from that same era, put words to what every other driver was already thinking. "There have been other tracks that separated the men from the boys. This is the track that will separate the brave from the weak after the boys are gone."[14]

Daytona appealed to fans as well as drivers. Like Darlington, Daytona afforded plenty of grandstand seats. In 1959, 42,000 people watched the first Daytona 500. Five years later, more than 70,000 fans were attending the race. Today, the grandstands at Daytona hold 140,000.

The success at Daytona quickly inspired others. The following year, 1960, construction began on three new superspeedways: Atlanta, Charlotte, and Hanford (California). Then, in 1969, Big Bill France raised the bar again. He completed a new superspeedway, the spectacular Talladega.

Talladega

Talladega stretched the imagination. At 2.66 miles long, it was the longest and soon the fastest speedway. It was here that Bill Elliott drove the fastest lap in NASCAR history—212 mph. Drivers, once they built experience, began racing here at speeds in excess of 200 mph. Because Talladega is wide (one lane wider than Daytona), racing three abreast became the norm. The intensity of competition racheted up several levels.

At last, racers had found a track that was built for speeds faster than most were comfortable driving. NASCAR had finally answered its own question: Just how fast is fast enough? Today, at Talladega and Daytona, NASCAR's rules require cars to install restrictor plates between the carburetor and manifold, reducing horsepower and slowing the cars.

The Decline of Short Tracks

The 1960s became the decade of superspeedways. With each passing season, the new big tracks—tracks with big attendance, big purses, and big action—got most of the attention. The pendulum was shifting away from short tracks, a change that was already evident when the R.J. Reynolds Tobacco Company entered the sport.

R.J. Reynolds burst onto the NASCAR scene in 1971. The federal government had banned television advertising of tobacco products, and the industry was searching for alternative ways to reach consumers. When first Ford and then Chevrolet announced they were pulling back from sponsoring stock car racing, the economic vacuum was quickly filled by tobacco companies.

In its first year with NASCAR, Reynolds agreed to sponsor a 500-mile race, which it named the Winston 500, at Talladega. In addition, the company posted a $100,000 bonus to be shared at the end of the season by NASCAR's top drivers. Only races of 250 miles or longer counted toward the prize money, and longer races usually meant larger tracks. Thus, the award, which became known as the Winston Cup, tended to favor larger tracks, which in turn meant more fans, more exposure.

The following year, in 1972, R.J. Reynolds proposed a deal: it would sponsor NASCAR's top racing series if NASCAR would reduce the number of races from forty-six to thirty-one. Reynolds believed that a shorter tour, profiling bigger events, would create more meaningful exposure and a more cost-efficient use of its promotion dollars. NASCAR agreed to the proposal, and thereafter its premier race series was known as the Winston Cup.

Which races were cut to accommodate Reynolds? Primarily the ones held at short tracks. In all, sixteen races were eliminated from thirteen different short tracks. Many were raceways that had signed up for NASCAR events in the earliest years; among them were Hickory Speedway, Columbia Speedway, and Greenville-Pickens. In addition to their length, all the tracks had one other common trait: They typically attracted no more than 5,000 people for a NASCAR event. The short tracks at Bristol and Richmond were left on the schedule in 1972, largely because their facilities held more people (Bristol, 25,000; Richmond, 15,000).

The 1972 season was run on twenty superspeedways, two road courses, and nine short tracks. The attendance at the nine short-track races totaled 200,000—an average of better than 22,000 per event. Although 240,000 had attended twenty-four short-track races the year before, the average for each event had been only 10,000. In one year, the R.J. Reynolds Company had reached its goal of increasing its sponsorship exposure on a per-event basis. With a limited schedule, more fans were now attending each race. And Reynolds was getting more bang for its promotion bucks.

The Business of Operating a Racetrack

The track is the arena. Like a football field or a ballpark, it is where all the teams come to play on the same day at the same time. Tracks are grouped into three categories: superspeedways (more than one mile), short tracks (less than one mile), and road courses (several miles long). Today, there are over 100 NASCAR-sanctioned racetracks, of all sizes, located in forty states.

Racetracks are owned and operated by individuals or major corporations, not by NASCAR. Throughout the year, a track owner may promote several different events at the track, including auto shows, car auctions, driving schools, and concerts. But without question, the primary business of a racetrack is to promote races. That is where the most money is made.

Whenever a NASCAR race is held at a track, the track owner pays a sanctioning fee. For this fee, NASCAR and its officials manage the race for the track owner. In return, the owner is able to advertise that the track is holding a NASCAR race. In other words, NASCAR puts on the race, and the track owner puts on the event.

Among the several revenue sources available to track owners are:

- General admission and luxury suites.
- Television and radio broadcast fees.
- Sponsorship fees and advertising.
- Concession, program, and merchandise sales.
- Hospitality tents and souvenir trailers.

Owners' expenses at a racetrack include:

- Sanctioning fee.
- Prize money.
- Operating costs.

Revenues

The business of owning and managing a racetrack is very much the same today as it was fifty years ago. The name of the game is to sell tickets.

Ticket prices vary, depending on the track, the event, and the type of accommodation. Fans have their choice of watching a race from a seat in the grandstands, from high above the track in luxurious air-conditioned suites, or from atop a recreational vehicle parked in the infield.

A reserved grandstand seat at Darlington Raceway for the Southern 500, for example, costs $95. Grandstand seats for the Daytona 500 are sold out years in advance, but if you could get one, it would run you somewhere between $60 and $175. That same seat for the Pepsi 400, which runs over the July 4th weekend, costs between $35 and $110. Support races, such as a Busch Grand National race on the Saturday before a Sunday Winston Cup race, generally cost between $40 and $90 at Daytona and $35 at Darlington.

Luxury suites are usually leased for a full year at a set price, which varies according to the track and the size of the suite. For example, at Daytona, suites range from $40,000 to $133,000 for the year. Each one includes TV monitors and private bathrooms; during a race, a full bar is installed and a catered meal is served. Suite owners get reserved parking for themselves and their guests. Each suite contains between forty and one hundred seats, so the suite holder has the opportunity to entertain as many as a hundred special guests every time a race is held at the track. Corporations that actively entertain prospects and VIP customers are usually the first to compete for open suites; most consider it an exceptionally good deal.

Finally, admission revenues also include tickets sold for parking and camping in the infield. The infield, that large open area encircled by the track, is the favorite spot for many of the most enthusiastic fans, who come with the whole family in a recreational vehicle outfitted for camping. Typically, slots in the infield are sold as a weekend block, so fans can enjoy three days of qualifying runs, practice runs, and races, along with barbecues, music, and boisterous fun. The cost varies according to location and event, but, generally speaking, a recreational vehicle can park for the weekend at Darlington for $175 plus $75 per person.

The combined revenues from grandstand seats, suites, and infield parking account for almost 70 percent of the track's revenue. They form, by far, the largest single source of cash for the owner. Not surprisingly, selling tickets, year in and year out, is the business priority at each track.

But there are several additional ways to generate revenue at each race. Inside the track, concessions (food and beverage) and souvenir sales (T-shirts, caps, and so on) produce about 5 percent of the track's revenue. Hospitality tents and souvenir trailers located on the property that surrounds the track pay rental fees of up to $5,000 a day, and sometimes must sign over a percentage of their souvenir sales as well (generally, 5 to 10 percent). Together, these account for another 5 percent of overall track revenue. Sponsorship, advertising, signage, and race programs, combined, account for about 10 percent of a track's revenue. Broadcast rights, primarily from television, contribute an equal amount.

Operating Expenses

The costs of running a track are rather simple. A track owner pays a sanctioning fee to NASCAR, prize money to the drivers and owners, and the operating expenses for entertaining 100,000 people.

It is no small chore to promote and host a NASCAR Winston Cup weekend. Although NASCAR manages the race itself, the track owner is responsible for everything beyond the racetrack walls, including adequate parking space and getting the fans smoothly into and out of the track grounds. Inside the track, the owner makes sure there is enough food, beverages, programs, and souvenirs for every-one, as well as clean restrooms, security, and first aid.

On average, there is approximately one track employee for every seventy-five race fans. For the big events at Darlington, Jim Hunter, the president of the raceway, hires about 1,000 people, who will work a ten-hour day. Hunter's counterpart at Daytona, John Graham, employs over 2,000 people to manage a weekend crowd of 150,000. In all, operating costs consume about 25 percent of a track's total expenses.

The balance, some 75 percent of a track's expense, goes toward prize money and sanctioning fees. Sanctioning fees vary, depending on the size of the event. Smaller tracks might pay NASCAR a sanc-tioning fee of approximately $150,000; larger superspeedways might pay $500,000.

The prize money for each event has three components: the race purse, television awards, and qualifying and special awards. Most of the qualifying and special awards are paid by sponsors, as we saw earlier; one exception is the Winners' Circle awards program, which is paid by the track owner. In a complex formula based on the prior year's standings, cash awards are made to the teams that did well in the previous year. The philosophy behind the Winners' Circle pro-gram says much about the NASCAR way of thinking. The original intent of the award was to provide economic support for the older, established teams to continue to compete, even if their recent per-formance had slipped, and to prevent new money from taking over the sport.

The television awards portion of prize money is an expense for track owners, but in fact the money comes from the fees paid to the track by the television network for the privilege of broadcasting the race. The track negotiates its own television broadcast rights, pays 10 percent of the receipts to NASCAR, and puts 25 percent into a fund to be divided among the drivers. This provides analysts the most common way to know what the broadcast rights were for any particular race: Calculate backward from the television award fund. For example, at the 1997 Daytona 500, the drivers shared a television award of $1.6 million. That meant the broadcast rights for the race were $6.4 million. After paying NASCAR 10 percent ($640,000) and awarding the racers the $1.6 million, the track owners pocketed a tidy $4.1 million in broadcast profits.

The race purse itself is a track expense and comes from ticket sales and concession profits. The dollar amount of the purse is set by the track owner and generally reflects the size of the track. Facilities with more seats draw in more revenues, and there is an expectation among drivers and team owners that the size of the purse will rise accordingly. NASCAR itself, with its strong tradition of fairness, has the same expectation, and works closely with track owners to encourage purses that are reasonable and fair to all.

The 1997 Daytona 500 race purse was $1.2 million, so the total prize money at the Daytona 500 was $4.3 million: $1.5 million in special awards, $1.6 million in television awards, and a $1.2 million race purse.

Overall, the business of operating a track can be very profitable. A major Winston Cup race held at a large facility generates approximately $10 million in revenue.[15] Direct expenses total approximately $5 to $6 million. Despite the heavy cost of personnel, it is not unusual for a racetrack to generate 50 to 60 percent operating margins, with net margins of 30 to 40 percent. These are very attractive economic returns for any business but, as we will see, they are also critical for the sport's future. If NASCAR is going to continue to grow, it must enter new markets and build new tracks. But the cost of building a new superspeedway currently approaches $100 million. Track owners cannot be expected to take that kind of capital risk unless promoting races continues to provide high returns.

The Business of Building a Racetrack

Fifty years ago, it was much easier to build a racetrack than it is now. It took money, certainly, but land far away from urban areas was cheap, and the fans weren't too fussy about expensive amenities. The most important asset was determination, and entrepreneurs like Harold Brasington at Darlington, H. Clay Earles at Martinsville, and Enoch Staley at North Wilkesboro were packed full of true grit. Today, track builders still need determination, but they also need a great deal of money and some form of government cooperation and assistance.

"Motorsports is a spectator industry," counsels Rick Horrow. "In order to compete for spectators, tracks must provide the same level of service and quality as any of the best sports stadiums in the country."[16] Horrow knows what he is talking about. He teaches sports law at Harvard University and runs a consulting firm that has provided advice and guidance to all the major sports leagues including the NFL, NBA, and MLB. Horrow is currently working with International Speedway Corporation as it pursues new track locations. The analysis they use reveals much about the economics of owning and managing a racetrack.

The first step in deciding where to build a track is not too difficult. Start with a list of the top twenty-five designated markets, then eliminate the potential sites that already have a major track within a 200- or 300-mile radius. Collect market and demographic information about those that remain, and solicit preliminary statements of interest from government and business leaders.

From this information, a short list is formed and then meetings are planned. "We never begin talking about the sport of stock car racing," explains Horrow. "In new markets, there is often a lack of awareness about NASCAR. But the job is made much easier when we first concentrate on the economic impact of NASCAR.

"We start by sharing our research with the local city government," Horrow says. "We know that race fans on average travel 300 miles to come to a race, they stay for two to three days and spend approximately $280 per day." For a speedway that accommodates 100,000 fans (a conservative estimate), the impact on the local economy would be $70 million for each major event.

Horrow's numbers appear valid. The city of Charlotte, North Carolina, estimates that fans generate over $70 million for its community during the Coca-Cola 600 Winston Cup race held at Charlotte Motor Speedway. At Darlington Raceway, which holds only 75,000 fans, the economic impact on the local level is $52 million during the Southern 500.[17]

To put this in perspective, the economic impact of one Winston Cup race weekend to a community is greater than that contributed by college basketball's Final Four, and it closely resembles the NFL Super Bowl numbers. In other words, argues Horrow, "A community with a large racetrack that hosts at least one NASCAR Winston Cup event a year receives the same impact as a Super Bowl and [the city] does not run the risk of having a losing team, waiting for its turn to host a Super Bowl, or worse, [having] a team's owner move the local franchise to another city." That argument wakes up city officials.

"The next step," Horrow continues, "is to educate officials about NASCAR." That, he claims, is the easy part. "I have had the opportunity to work with all major sports and many individual organizations in the past fifteen years, but I fervently believe the France family and NASCAR are the most enlightened and analytically wise groups in all major sports. Skeptical business leaders are favorably impressed when the France family shows up. The Frances translate so well what is special about this industry."

Once the NASCAR concept is sold, the next step is to help the community understand what a modern-day track demands from the local infrastructure. Officials of most major cities understand quite well the requirements of other sports' structures. Basketball arenas seat between 18,000 and 20,000. A baseball field like Coors Field or Camden Yards holds between 45,000 and 50,000 fans. An NFL football stadium must have 65,000 seats—or 75,000, if a city wishes to host a Super Bowl. However, today's NASCAR tracks are built on the concept of 100,000 seats and up. The numbers are extraordinary. One look at the new Texas superspeedway that debuted in 1997 tells the whole story.

Northwest of Dallas–Fort Worth, nestled on 1,000 acres adjoining Ross Perot's Alliance Airport, sits Texas Motor Speedway (TMS). It took twenty months to build the 1.5-mile track with grandstands that hold 150,061 race fans. Another 50,000 fans can fit in the infield. There are 2,450 restrooms (the most in the world, for an enclosed facility), and eight acres are set aside for handicapped parking. To give fans seated in the lower grandstands a clear view of the backstretch, the infield was lowered. Positioned high above the track, in rows of two, are 208 luxury suites, each of which holds 60 guests. For those who don't like traffic jams, there are twenty helipads. Adjacent to the track is the eleven-story Lone Star Tower, with sixty-seven condominiums priced at $575,000 each.

Just how big is Texas Motor Speedway? You can fit eight 65,000-seat Texas Stadiums inside the track.

The first Winston Cup race at the new speedway was the Interstate Batteries 500, on April 6, 1997. Tickets went on sale January 18. Within ten days, all 50,000 infield tickets, priced at $50 each, had been sold, and so had all the 150,000 grandstand seats, at prices ranging from $5 to $80. The luxury suites, priced between $65,000 and $100,000, are being snapped up as well. CBS paid a reported $4 million for the rights to broadcast the inaugural race—something of a bargain, considering the race drew a 6.6 rating, the highest rated NASCAR event on any network excluding the Daytona 500.

In the future, will all new tracks be like Texas Motor Speedway? Probably not. Bruton Smith, chairman of Speedway Motor Sports, which owns TMS, has a reputation for huge statements. His Charlotte Motor Speedway was the first superspeedway to hold night NASCAR Winston Cup racing and the first to build track-side condominiums. (Most observers thought this idea the most foolhardy venture they had ever heard of—who wants to live right next to a racetrack—but it was a resounding success. Smith later commented that his only mistake was pricing them too low.)

However, even though Texas Motor Speedway may never be topped by a larger track, it has set a standard in spectator enjoyment. It wasn't easy to move 200,000 fans in and out of Texas Motor Speedway for its first event, especially since heavy rainstorms had prevented completion of paving work and left the parking lot ankle-deep in mud. In a last-minute scramble, speedway officials set up a system of satellite parking areas and shuttle buses.

Once inside the track, fans were treated to new levels of comfort. All the bleacher bench seats had backrests, and 36,000 premium seats had theater-style armrests, a luxury previously unheard of in racing. Twenty-one elevators moved fans to and from their tower seats, and when they went out to the concourse for a snack or a restroom break, closed-circuit television monitors allowed them to keep up with the race action.

The cost of building a modern track that can hold at least 100,000 fans is well over $100 million. It was reported that Texas Motor Speedway cost between $120 and $140 million. Roger Penske's new California Speedway, located in Fontana in southern California, cost $105 million. Like Bruton Smith at Texas Motor Speedway, Penske has set new standards in track amenities and service.

At California Speedway, guests (they are not called fans) are greeted by customer service ambassadors wearing special high-visibility vests, who can give directions to seats, ATM machines, or a place to change your baby's diaper. Three hundred Boy Scouts and Girl Scouts circulate on tidy patrol, making sure no trash is left on the ground. Children who come to the race are given plastic wristbands with their name, address, section and seat number. To help pass the time until the race starts, each child receives a speedway coloring book and pencils. Public drunkenness, profanity, and offensive signs are strictly banned.

Adding grandstand capacity to existing track facilities runs between $350 and $400 per seat. This includes not only the cost of building a grandstand but the cost for additional parking, restrooms, and other ancillary services. Most tracks can recover their costs for new seats within four to five major events. New speedways, however, average between $1,000 and $1,500 per seat, because of the cost of acquiring the land, constructing a new track, and building all the facilities. A new track needs ten to fifteen major events to recoup its investment.

Still, with the kind of economic numbers being achieved at many tracks across the country, it is hard to find a downside. Weather is always a concern. Stock cars don't race in the rain, and races can be delayed or even postponed. But passionate race fans are seldom denied. The 1997 Talladega Winston 500 was postponed twice be-cause of rain, but all 140,000 fans still showed up the next weekend to watch the race. Even broadcast fees are guaranteed, good weather or bad.

As long as a track can continue to promote meaningful events such as NASCAR racing, profit margins and return on investments will remain attractive. So what could go wrong? The one challenge faced by every major racetrack, old and new, big and small, is getting and keeping a NASCAR Winston Cup date.

Who Decides the NASCAR Schedule?

Every year, the races that make up each NASCAR racing series— Winston Cup, Busch Grand National, Craftsman Truck, and the rest—are awarded to specific tracks. It is a one-year agreement be-tween NASCAR and the track, and there is no automatic renewal; the schedule for each series is set anew each year. Who makes the decision? Just one individual: Bill France, Jr.

Like his father before him, France has the final word on which tracks get which races on which dates. With so much power in the hands of one person, the situation is ripe for unscrupulous behavior. That such behavior is unknown says a great deal about the sport, the NASCAR organization, and the France family ethic.

Most investment professionals are familiar with the term "Chinese Wall." In investment banking firms, it designates the in-visible barrier between the research department, which produces background information on companies, and investment bankers, who raise capital for these companies based on the research reports. That barrier maintains a level of objectivity in what could otherwise become a self-serving information loop.

In the same way, there exists a Chinese Wall between NASCAR, which assigns the extremely valuable Winston Cup dates to racetracks, and International Speedway Corporation, which owns and manages several tracks. Without that barrier of objectivity, NASCAR, in the person of Bill France, could easily award the best dates to ISC tracks, to the unfair benefit of the France family, which owns 60 percent of ISC.

NASCAR's Chinese Wall is built on a strong foundation: the tradition of loyalty and the sense of fairness that characterize the Frances, the organization, and the sport of stock car racing. That strong sense of integrity binds together all the elements of the sport, overcoming temporary strife and personality conflicts.

It is not simply empty sloganeering: NASCAR matches its actions to its words. For evidence, consider the final race on the Winston Cup circuit. In sheer drama, nothing matches it; the season's winner is often determined in that last race. Excitement is high, attendance is high, profits are high. And the last race is, by NASCAR tradition, held each year at Atlanta Motor Speedway, which is owned by Bruton Smith's Speedway Motor Sports. Bill France has the power to deny his rival this plum, but he does not.

When Bill France draws up the schedule each year, track owners have the right to decline a race date from NASCAR, but such thinking is unheard of. Considering the dollars involved in a Winston Cup race, coupled with the scarcity of dates, no track owner would ever risk turning down an invitation from NASCAR.

Even though theoretically the schedule could change at any time, in fact the NASCAR Winston Cup schedule changes very little. Part of the reason is tradition: certain races are historically linked with certain dates. The Mountain Dew Southern 500 always runs at Darlington on Labor Day; Charlotte Motor Speedway's Coca-Cola 600 is always run during Memorial Day weekend. But there is also another reason why race dates change very little, and it has to do with the history of the sport.

The one human characteristic that best defines NASCAR and the France family, I believe, is loyalty. In the earliest years of the sport, before television and before million-dollar corporate sponsorships, NASCAR was built largely on the sacrifice and dedication of a few families who risked their own money to build a racetrack. The France family acknowledges this sacrifice, and reciprocates by protecting the interests of those families, making sure the older tracks still get their Winston Cup dates. Since 1972, only five tracks have been dropped from the NASCAR Winston Cup schedule. It is not the most economically efficient way to allocate race dates, but it is an approach to business that has become a hallmark of the NASCAR way.

That being the case, how does NASCAR grow? With bigger tracks being built and bigger markets beckoning, NASCAR must find ways to balance the demands for the future with its sense of responsibility. To date, achieving that balance has meant exerting its influence behind the scenes to ensure that whenever a track loses a Winston Cup slot, the track owner is compensated in some fashion. One other obvious solution is to add more race dates.

Ever since RJR Nabisco entered the sport, there has been a general unwillingness to expand the race schedule from its current level. For the 1997 season, one Winston Cup race was added, which brings the series to thirty-two races, but everyone agrees that there is no likelihood of returning to earlier days when a series comprised forty or fifty events. Partly this is a question of marketing strategy; the notion that a limited schedule increases the value of individual events is still highly regarded. Partly it is sheer practicality; it is becoming increasingly difficult to squeeze in extra race dates.

The NASCAR season runs from February to November. In 1997, there were thirty-two Winston Cup points races and two nonpoints

NASCAR events (Busch Clash and Winston Select). That left only seven open weekends with no racing. Open weekends are used to reschedule races that were postponed because of weather, or for test runs. Each team is allowed seven sessions during the season to test its equipment at different tracks, and every team takes full advantage of this opportunity. But even if the amount of testing were curtailed— and there are those who argue for doing so—the NASCAR season, as currently constructed, has little room for expansion.

New track owners, then, cannot pin their hopes for getting a Winston Cup date on the possibility of an expanded schedule. Their next logical step is to buy a track that already has a Winston Cup date and then work to move that date to their new track. It is a strategy that now is unfolding.

When Enoch Staley passed away in May 1995, his family decided to sell the racetrack he had built at North Wilkesboro. A ⅝-mile track nestled in the Blue Ridge Mountains of North Carolina, North Wilkesboro is one of NASCAR's oldest tracks and the traditional site of two Winston Cup races. Instead of upgrading the aging facility, the Staley family decided it was time to retrieve the capital they had invested in the track for fifty years. They put out the word that the track was for sale.

Bruton Smith, president of Speedway Motor Sports, and Bob Bahre, who owns New Hampshire International Speedway, each purchased 50 percent. Smith took one of the North Wilkesboro race dates for his new Texas Motor Speedway. Bahre took the other and added it to his New Hampshire track, making it his second Winston Cup date.

It was a convenient way to deal with a difficult situation. North Wilkesboro, although rich with NASCAR history, was unable to keep up with NASCAR's accelerated growth. But instead of the Staley family being pushed out, capitalism solved the problem for all.

NASCAR moved two Winston Cup dates to larger facilities, one of them a brand-new market (Dallas–Fort Worth), and the Staley family pocketed $12 million.

The Value of a Winston Cup Date

The purchase of North Wilkesboro set in motion an idea that previously had not been given much attention: that a Winston Cup *date* has marketable value, separate from the assets of a racetrack itself. Smith and Bahre own the racetrack at North Wilkesboro, but the track has sat idle since its sale; there is no racing. In one sense, then, the sale of the track helps to establish a market value for a Winston Cup race—or, more correctly, the value of a Winston Cup weekend. Because a NASCAR Winston Cup date includes a support race on Saturday, its value should include the support race profits as well.

Although larger NASCAR Winston Cup events earn $8 million before tax, a smaller track like North Wilkesboro probably earned about $2 million pretax per event, with the support race bringing in an additional $500,000. Both Smith and Bahre purchased North Wilkesboro for approximately two times its net profits before tax. Compared to the prices now being quoted for racetracks, they got a bargain.

There are a few independent family-owned tracks left with Winston Cup dates. The Sawyer family owns Richmond; the Mattioli family owns Pocono; the Clay Earles family owns Martinsville; and the DeWitt family owns Rockingham. Each track currently receives two Winston Cup dates each year, and each family has been courted by potential buyers.

The Mattioli family and the Sawyer family have repeatedly denied any interest in selling their tracks. Bruton Smith offered the Clay

Earles family $30 million for Martinsville, which was turned down. The track at Rockingham was the prize in a recent joust between Bruton Smith and Roger Penske, whose company, Penske Motorsports, owns the new California Speedway as well as Michigan and Nazareth Speedways. Penske had an option agreement with the DeWitt family to purchase 65 percent of the track for $27 million. Smith, who already owned 25 percent of the track, countered with $72 million for full ownership. In May 1977, Carrie DeWitt smiled on suitor Penske, accepting his 65 percent option for $26.5 million in Penske Motorsports stock. Penske now controls two more Winston Cup dates. Those two races earn pretax $5 million a year at Rockingham but could bring in over $20 million at a larger facility.

With more transactions and more offers, owners are beginning to get a sense of the value of their tracks. The price of racetracks is on the rise. If we apply conventional cash flow multiples that are used to value other types of businesses, the value of racetracks could be headed even higher. Using a conservative multiple of eight for valuation purposes, a major track with two Winston Cup event weekends per year might be worth $160 million. In that case, building a huge new facility like Texas Motor Speedway ($120 million or more) or California Speedway ($105 million) is a smart investment only if the tracks get awarded two NASCAR dates per year.

No one knows exactly what will happen next, but one thing is certain: The NASCAR landscape is sure to change over the next few years. The change will come with new tracks in new markets. NASCAR is experiencing a growth spurt that requires the sport to take advantage of these new opportunities. As a consequence, the NASCAR Winston Cup schedule cannot stay the same. Already, tracks like Walt Disney World Speedway, Pike's Peak Raceway, and Homestead Motorsports Complex are actively soliciting for Winston Cup events. International Speedway, Penske Motorsports, and

Speedway Motorsports are searching for new locations. Potential track sites in Chicago, Denver, Sacramento, and Kansas City are under consideration. The transition from older tracks in smaller markets to newer tracks in larger markets will not be painless, but neither should it be penniless.

Investing in NASCAR

With NASCAR's surging popularity and strong financial success, many investors are looking for ways to participate in the boom. Because NASCAR itself is a private company owned and controlled by the France family, there is no way for investors to benefit from NASCAR directly. However, five publicly traded companies give investors the opportunity to become co-owners of racing-related businesses, including some of NASCAR's most popular tracks.*

1. International Speedway Corporation (ISC) trades in the NASDAQ National Market, under the symbol ISCA.† ISC, headquartered in Daytona Beach, Florida, owns and operates Daytona International Speedway, Talladega Superspeedway, Darlington Raceway, Watkins Glen International, Phoenix, and Tucson Raceway Park. It also owns DAYTONA USA, a motorsports entertainment

---

*In connection with the Private Securities Litigation Reform Act of 1995, the author wishes to inform readers that there are many factors that can cause a company's actual results to differ from the material presented in this book. It is prudent for all investors to conduct their own research and to reach their own conclusions about a company before investing.

†Robert Hagstrom is portfolio manager of Focus Trust, a no-load mutual fund. Focus Trust owns shares in International Speedway Corporation. In the future, Focus Trust may purchase or sell shares in International Speedway as well as other companies mentioned in this book.

complex attached to the Daytona speedway; MRN, the Motor Racing Network; and 12 percent of Penske Motorsports. ISC is 60 percent owned by the France family.

2. Penske Motorsports also trades in the NASDAQ National Market, under the stock symbol SPWY. Led by the legendary Roger Penske, it is headquartered in Detroit. Penske owns and operates Michigan International Speedway, North Carolina Motorspeedway (Rockingham), and Nazareth Motor Speedway in Pennsylvania. In 1997, Penske completed construction of California Speedway, an 80,000-seat track located in southern California, which hosted its first Winston Cup event on June 22, 1997.

Penske Motorsports also sells motorsports-related merchandise, including caps and T-shirts, and Goodyear racing tires purchased by the Winston Cup race teams. Approximately 70 percent of the company's revenues come from racetrack admissions; 30 percent is attributed to merchandise, accessories, and racing tires.

3. Speedway Motorsports Incorporated became a publicly traded company in 1995. The stock trades on the New York Stock Exchange, under the symbol TRK. Since taking his company public, Bruton Smith, chairman and chief executive officer, has been aggressively purchasing racetracks. The company began with two tracks: Charlotte Motor Speedway and Atlanta Motor Speedway. After the initial public offering, in 1996 Speedway Motorsports purchased Bristol Motor Speedway, one of NASCAR's famous short tracks, located in east Tennessee, and Sears Point Raceway, a road course in northern California.

Speedway Motorsports also owns Texas Motor Speedway, our country's second largest sports facility, located near Dallas–Fort Worth. The 1.5-mile quad-oval track is lighted, which allows the track to promote night racing. It is also dual-banked, permitting the track to host both stock car and Indy car racing. NASCAR's Winston Cup cars race on the high bank; Indy cars, which are faster, run safely on the lower bank. Speedway Motorsports also manufactures and distributes Legends Cars, twin-cylinder ⅝-scale versions of NASCAR's modified cars, complete with a full roll cage and safety harness for drivers.

4. Soon after Speedway Motorsports issued shares, Dover Downs International Speedway, a one-mile track located in Delaware, was taken public by Merrill Lynch. Dover Downs, symbol DVD, like Speedway Motorsports, trades on the New York Stock Exchange. But unlike Speedway Motorsports, Dover Downs owns only one track. However, it generates additional revenue from harness racing and gambling: pari-mutuel betting on simulcast horse racing and video lottery (slot) machines. In fact, 70 percent of Dover Downs's revenues comes from gaming; motorsports provide 30 percent.

5. To date, no Winston Cup racing team has gone public. Roger Penske's racing teams, both CART and Winston Cup, are not part of Penske Motorsports; they are separately held in a private company. You may not be able to own shares in Hendrick Motorsports or Richard Childress Racing, but you can own shares in the company that distributes miniatures of their cars. Action Performance Companies (symbol ACTN on the NASDAQ National Market) designs and markets collectible-quality die-cast model cars that are exact replicas of motorsports vehicles.

The stock market has created opportunities for all these companies. First, each company was able to tap investors for capital that, in turn, was used to expand operations. Speedway Motorsports used its public offering to build Texas Motor Speedway.

Penske Motorsports used its offering to build the California Speedway. Recently, International Speedway raised $80 million in a sec-
ondary offering so the company would be in a position to build or
partner a new track in a new market.

The stock market has created another additional benefit for
NASCAR racing: wider recognition for the sport. Five years ago,
International Speedway was the only public company in this
group; no major brokerage firm or analyst followed it. Kevin Daly,
at Hoefer & Arnett in San Francisco, was one of the few analysts
to pound the table about International Speedway and NASCAR.
But since that time, more brokerage firms have begun to cover the
sport and these companies. From Merrill Lynch in New York to
Wheat First Securities in Richmond, to J.C. Bradford & Company
in Nashville, and to Montgomery Securities in San Francisco, all
have jumped on the bandwagon. Today, because of customer demand, Wall Street can no longer ignore NASCAR.

Nor can it ignore performance. International Speedway, which
sold for less than $50 per share in 1993, reached $300 per share at
the end of 1996, and split fifteen-for-one.

Racetracks—Sports Stadiums of the 21st Century

It would be a mistake to assume a racetrack cannot survive without
a NASCAR Winston Cup event. Racing is very profitable, and
most tracks across the country do very well booking some sort of
race each weekend. Even Nashville Speedway, which once hosted a
Winston Cup event, continues to thrive by promoting Busch Grand
National, Craftsman Truck, and Late Model races.

All tracks are well advised to promote different series for their fans as a complement to the big events. Some tracks take this notion further by promoting other events unrelated to motorsports, such as rock concerts. While there is nothing wrong with this strategy, the forward thinking argues that if racing is the magnet, tracks should provide entertainment that is synergistic to the sport. At its most fully developed level, that thinking means transforming racetracks into tourist attractions. And here again, the France family leads the way.

DAYTONA USA

DAYTONA USA is a motorsports entertainment complex attached to the Daytona Superspeedway. It is the brainchild of Lesa France Kennedy, executive vice president of International Speedway Corporation (and daughter of Bill France, Jr.), who, like her father and her grandfather, knows how to recognize an opportunity. "Race fans were always stopping by the speedway for a peek," she recalls. "Once here, they wanted to purchase souvenirs and take a quick tour. But we were never set up to handle this type of demand."[18]

Close to 500,000 tourists—not counting the crowds who arrive for race weekends—travel to world-famous Daytona International Speedway each year. As she began envisioning the project, Kennedy asked those fans, through an in-depth survey, what they wanted from an entertainment facility. Before presenting the final plans to her father, she asked the same questions of all track employees, race drivers, and team owners.

The end result is a spectacular interactive entertainment motorsports attraction. At DAYTONA USA, race fans are invited to participate in a live NASCAR Winston Cup pit stop. Through numerous computer-simulated races, fans can race one another. They can tour a museum that catalogs the sport's history from birth. Using interactive computer consoles, they can ask questions of their favorite drivers. Or they can watch a movie called *Daytona 500*, presented on a screen fifty-five feet wide and twenty-six feet tall, with an eight-channel DTS sound system that pounds with all the excitement of an actual race.

In the sports world, DAYTONA USA has become the entertainment model. According to Rick Horrow, the NFL and Major League Baseball are currently studying the facility, with an eye to whether this concept will work for their own stadiums. The idea of creating a facility that will attract fans to the stadium even on days when events are not held makes eminent good sense.

But International Speedway Corporation and NASCAR are already far out ahead of the curve. DAYTONA USA was positioned to succeed from the start. Using the formula they have employed so brilliantly in the past, Kennedy and ISC, early on, lined up corporate sponsors for the facility. Chevrolet, Ford, Pontiac, DuPont, Pepsi, Gatorade, Goodyear, STP, Western Auto's Parts America, and Circuit City paid a total of more than $10 million for the right to call themselves founding sponsors of DAYTONA USA.

Sunset Raceway

If DAYTONA USA shows us the future of NASCAR, Sunset Raceway in Nebraska symbolizes the best of its still-vital traditions. When I walked into Sunset Raceway on a Sunday night in May, my instincts about stock car racing were reaffirmed. Sunset is a ⅜-mile dirt track west of Omaha. It is part of the Winston Racing series that features Late Model, Grand National, and Pro-Am events.

It was cool and windy, not a perfect night for racing. But none of the 5,000 or so fans in the grandstands seemed to mind. Even though most had to be up early the next morning for work or school, no one was leaving until the last event was over.

On a dirt track like this—small, tidy, but not flashy—it's easy to find yourself thinking back on stock car history. Before anything else, there first had to be track owners. Without a track to race on, drivers were no more than moonshine runners and back-street dragsters. Without people like Harold Brasington, there could not have been a Richard Petty. It was the track promoter who gave drivers not only a track to run on but a stadium in which to perform in front of thousands of fans. Today's celebrated drivers owe their fame and fortune to those few entrepreneurs who, without government taxes and subsidies, risked their own personal fortune to realize a dream.

Tonight, Craig Kelley, co-owner of the track, was upstairs tallying the night's profits. Most of his 5,200 grandstand seats had been sold, at $10 a seat. In the best tradition of Harold Brasington, Kelley is a smart promoter. His track is well run, well attended, and profitable. He was looking forward to a good season.

Meanwhile, the fans were eagerly awaiting the last race of the night, a twenty-five-lap sprint race. Soon the Late Model cars began slowly circling the track, waiting for the green flag. Suddenly, the announcer's voice blared through the loudspeaker: "Ladies and gentlemen, please rise and salute your driver." All 5,000 fans stood as one, waving and cheering as the cars drove by.

Then I witnessed something quite special: to a man, the drivers waved back. As they came around the fourth turn and headed down the frontstretch, all the drivers, from the two on the poles to the tail end of the line, waved to the crowd. The fans went wild, screaming even louder and reaching their waving arms out farther, as if to touch the drivers.

That brief exchange—a roar from the crowd and a friendly, cheerful response from the athletes—epitomized for me the aspect of stock car racing that sets it apart from all other sports: the unique relationship between fan and driver. It is a relationship built on admiration, respect, and affection that runs both ways. There is a deep sense of personal connection in NASCAR not felt in other sports. In that one moment, late on a cold Sunday night, we all felt warmed by that bond.

6

TRUE AMERICAN HEROES

THE YEAR WAS 1975. Tom Higgins, a reporter for the *Charlotte (NC) Observer*, was searching for a story for the upcoming World 600. Looking over the entry list, he spotted a name that sounded familiar—Dale Earnhardt. Higgins called the public relations office at Charlotte Motor Speedway. "Is this Dale Earnhardt related to Ralph Earnhardt?"[1] Ralph Earnhardt was a legendary short-track racer in the 1950s; if there was a connection, Higgins had his story.

"Yes, Dale is Ralph's boy. As a matter of fact, he's out here practicing right now."

Higgins hung up the phone, hopped in his car, and drove out to the speedway. He found young Dale Earnhardt working on his car along pit row. He was easy to spot. "He looked just like his daddy," Higgins remembered later, "tall and thin."

There was another reason Dale was easy to spot. "There were only three people at the track that day," Higgins recalled, "Dale, an ambulance driver [paramedic], and myself." The paramedic was there because the rules required it; anytime a driver practiced at the track, an ambulance and paramedic had to stand by. But there was no one else around, no crew chief, no crew. Just Dale and his car. He had pulled the stock car to the track on an open-bed trailer attached to his pickup truck.

Dale was aware of Higgins's arrival but continued to work on his car. "He was under it, then in it," said Higgins. "He would run a few laps and stop and make more adjustments. Just about the time he looked like he was loading up, I strolled over to introduce myself."

Dale was less than thrilled to see Higgins. He started shuffling his feet, looking off in the distance. Each question Higgins asked, the best Dale could do was "Nope" or "Yep." It was clear that Higgins wasn't getting the story he had hoped for. Then he had an idea.

"I put down my pad and pen, and then I told Dale I had seen his daddy race. That got a reaction."

Dale looked up. "Where did you see my daddy?"

"It was at McCormick Field in Asheville, North Carolina, in '58. I was a cub reporter then for the Asheville *Citizen Times*." McCormick Field had been an old minor league facility for the Brooklyn Dodgers, Higgins reminisced, "until they moved the team. After that, the town decided to lay a quarter-mile asphalt racetrack around the baseball diamond."

Dale was playing close attention. "Your daddy and Banjo Matthews started on the first row of that race." Banjo Matthews, a famous race driver and car builder, had been the local track favorite. He had won sixteen races in a row at McCormick. "After a few laps, they started banging on each other. Your daddy didn't take much more. He flipped Banjo over into McCormick centerfield."

Dale stared at Higgins, his eyes shining. "Damn, I heard about that race, but I've never talked to anyone who saw it. Tell me more."

"Well, half the crowd at McCormick was pulling for Banjo and half of them were pulling for your daddy. When Banjo flipped, it looked worse than it really was. The car was upside down, spinning around with smoke trailing out of it. They had to red flag the race to see if Banjo was all right. Dickie Plemmons, a Banjo protégé, got out of his race car and ran over to your daddy. When he poked his head inside and started yelling, your daddy slugged him and Dickie's head popped back. The grandstands almost broke into a riot."

Dale was laughing now. He loved to hear racing stories, particularly ones that involved his father.

NASCAR is a sport full of father–son combinations. Lee Petty, a Grand National Champion, is the father of Richard Petty, who became NASCAR's all-time racing champion with 200 victories and seven Winston Cup championships. Buck Baker, who won championships in 1956 and 1957, introduced his son Buddy to racing. Buddy Baker went on to claim forty poles and nineteen Winston Cup victories before being inducted into the National Motorsports Press Association and International Motorsports Halls of Fame. Ned Jarrett, the Grand National Champion who raced against Ralph Earnhardt at McCormick, is the father of Dale Jarrett, a perennial top ten driver and one of the most well-liked men in the sport.

The two men continued to talk about racing and the old days, and gradually Higgins tried to draw Dale out. At one point, he asked about Dale's ambitions. He needed a story. Higgins mentioned some of the father–son combinations and then asked Dale if he felt he was following in his father's footsteps.

"Dale began to shuffle his feet again and his eyes dropped back to the ground." He didn't seem to want to answer. Soon, the conversation trailed off, and Dale began to pack the trailer and load his car. Before he left, he turned toward Higgins and confessed, "I hope one day to make my daddy proud."

Ralph Earnhardt was the 1956 NASCAR Sportsman Champion, the equivalent of today's Busch Grand National Division. He won over 350 NASCAR races, mostly on short tracks around the Carolinas. Ned Jarrett, who was his contemporary, said, "Ralph Earnhardt was absolutely the toughest race driver I ever raced against. When you went to the track, you knew he was the man to beat."[2] "He was the kind of driver, if you raced him clean, he'd race you clean," said Jeff Hammond, crew chief for Darrell Waltrip. "But if you lay on him or beat on him, you better be prepared for one wild ride."[3] Ralph also gained a reputation for building good race cars. He installed roll bars in the driver's door and perfected tire stagger (using less air pressure and smaller tires on the left side to better handle the turns) when few others knew what it meant.

Ralph Earnhardt did well enough to support his wife Martha and their five children with his race winnings. They lived comfortably in a modest two-story white house in Kannapolis, North Carolina. Each night, after supper, while Martha put the kids to bed, Ralph Earnhardt walked out to his shop behind the house and worked on his race car. As a boy, Dale fell asleep listening to his father work on the engine.

Every day after school Dale would rush home to help out around the shop; when he got older, his father took him to the races. Even though he was too young to be allowed inside the pit area, once the race started, Dale would crawl up on the truck and watch his father race. Driving home to Kannapolis, late into the night, Ralph would talk about the race while Dale listened quietly to every word.

One late afternoon in 1973, Ralph Earnhardt suffered a massive heart attack while working in his shop. Dale, then twenty-two, found his father slumped over his race car. Ralph Earnhardt was forty-four.

Losing his father was a devastating blow for Dale. At the time Ralph died, Dale had only been racing dirt tracks for a year and a half—not enough time to show his father what he had learned. Dale struggled for many years, living hand to mouth and trying to save enough money to race. What little money he made didn't buy much equipment. Those who lent a hand often did so more for Ralph's boy than for Dale.

But he didn't give up. Racing brought Dale closer to his dad. "I'm sure his spirit rides with me in my race car, as sure of it as anything in the world."[4]

Finally, in 1975, after years of driving dirt tracks, Dale Earnhardt got a shot at the big time: the World 600 at Charlotte Motor Speedway. When Tom Higgins tracked him down for his interview, Dale was fine-tuning a 1974 Dodge owned by Ed Negre, a small independent owner; it was only a one-race deal. He would be racing against Richard Petty, Buddy Baker, Cale Yarborough, Darrell Waltrip, and David Pearson—the stars of NASCAR Winston Cup racing.

On May 25, some 90,000 fans jammed into Charlotte Motor Speedway to watch NASCAR's longest stock car race—600 miles. It took four hours to complete the event. Petty, Yarborough, and Pearson swapped the lead fifteen times before Richard Petty claimed another NASCAR victory. Yarborough took second, Pearson third. Dale finished twenty-second, forty-five laps behind Petty. While the winners celebrated at victory lane, Ralph's boy packed up his car and headed home.

After work one evening, I stopped by our neighborhood grocery store to pick up a few things. Dashing toward the checkout, I came to an abrupt stop when I caught sight of a familiar face. There at the end of the aisle, stacked high on top of one another, stood the display of bright orange cereal boxes. "The Breakfast of Champions," with a picture of Ralph's boy on it. Dale Earnhardt had become the first NASCAR driver to appear on a box of Wheaties.

Success did not come easily for Dale, any more than it does for other drivers. It takes years to break into Winston Cup racing. Dale returned to Charlotte twice in 1976 but failed to finish either race. The next year wasn't much better. Dale's big break came in 1978 when he drove one race for Rod Osterlund and finished fourth at Atlanta International Raceway. The following year, 1979, Dale drove a full season for Osterlund and was named Rookie of the Year. The next season, 1980, he became the Winston Cup Champion.

Ralph's boy has won over $30 million racing stock cars. He has also won seven NASCAR Winston Cup Championships, which ties him with Richard Petty. But nobody calls him Ralph's boy any more. He is Dale Earnhardt, arguably the greatest stock car driver of all time.[5]

Drivers and Deal Makers

Stock car drivers are independent contractors; they hire themselves out for the season to the best team possible. Each driver negotiates his own financial arrangement with the owner of his race team, so no two deals are alike. However, all drivers receive income from three basic sources: (1) racing, (2) personal endorsements, and (3) licensing revenue.

Prize Money

Earnings from racing have two facets: a base salary, plus a percentage of the winnings. Drivers who are just starting out at the Winston Cup level may get a salary of $100,000 and 10 percent of the purse. Those with more experience but no record of recent success may be able to negotiate something between $100,000 and $200,000 in salary and perhaps up to 20 percent of the winnings.

For NASCAR's top drivers, those who have years of experience and have demonstrated the ability to win races, salaries range between $500,000 and $800,000 a year, plus 30 to 50 percent of the winnings. In a season, a top ten driver will win between $1 million and $3 million for the team. The driver's take, on top of his salary, could be anywhere from $300,000 to $1.5 million.

Personal Endorsements

In NASCAR Winston Cup racing, drivers are allowed to negotiate their own personal endorsement packages. Sometimes, these deals work in conjunction with a team sponsorship. For example, Jeff Gordon has a personal services agreement with Pepsi, which also sponsors Hendrick Motorsports. But it is not unusual for a driver to endorse a product or service that is unrelated to the driver's team.

The total annual endorsement packages for top NASCAR drivers easily surpass their income from racing. In 1996, Dale Earnhardt's combined salary and prize winnings totaled $2.5 million but his endorsements earned him an additional $8 million.[6]

The financial package for endorsements, personal service agreements, and special appearances is on the rise for all NASCAR drivers. Dale Earnhardt, Jeff Gordon, Terry Labonte, and Dale Jarrett have become able pitchmen. They are comfortable in front of television cameras, which only increases their value to corporations. If you want to hire a top NASCAR driver to endorse your product, plan to spend as much as you would to get a top professional basketball, football, or baseball player. Today, you won't get Dale Earnhardt's attention until bidding reaches seven figures.

Licensing and Souvenir Sales

As NASCAR has become more popular nationwide, it has made several drivers famous. This is key, because fame is what creates the opportunity to generate licensing revenues. Drivers earn royalties from the sale of apparel (T-shirts, baseball caps, and the like), die-cast cars, trading cards, and other miscellaneous products: beach towels, mugs, key chains, stickers, flags, and banners. It represents a significant portion of their overall earnings.

NASCAR drivers have one important financial advantage not extended to stick-and-ball professional athletes: They control their own licensing and souvenir sales. This is an important distinction. Michael Jordan, Troy Aikman, and Cal Ripkin, Jr., may be the most popular athletes in their sport, but their licensing is controlled by their respective leagues. The National Basketball Association, the National Football League, and Major League Baseball have proper-ties divisions that sell uniforms, T-shirts, baseball caps, and other souvenirs to fans. The money from these sales is accumulated and then shared equally among all the athletes. Products with Michael Jordan's name outsell all those of other basketball players, but his paycheck from souvenir sales is the same as all the other players in the NBA. Top NASCAR drivers, in contrast, earn more from sou-venir sales than from racing.

Years ago, race teams and sponsors had no interest in souvenir sales; the business was tied solely to the driver. But with the explo-sive growth of NASCAR souvenir sales, teams and sponsors have retained part of their rights. Today, the typical souvenir relation-ship is designed to benefit the driver, the team, and the sponsor equally. Still, even after splitting the reward with their team and their sponsor, NASCAR drivers outmatch other professional ath-letes in souvenir benefits.

In the souvenir market, about 50 percent of total sales is from ap-parel, 25 percent from die-cast cars, 10 percent from trading cards, and 15 percent from miscellaneous items. The actual dollar earnings for drivers are difficult to uncover, but we may get a sense of their magnitude by looking at the top.

It is estimated that Dale Earnhardt—who is the Michael Jordan of stock car racing—accounts for 40 percent of the total NASCAR souvenir market. He is that popular.

Earnhardt, in fact, fully personifies the phenomenon of fan adoration translated into driver revenue. One recent incident explains why. In 1996, at Talladega, Dale crashed his car, broke his collarbone, and fractured his sternum. Two weeks later, in a qualifying run at Watkins Glen, he took the pole with a record time. When reporters asked him how he could do that—make a record run while injured—Earnhardt just smiled and said, "It hurts so good."

Within hours, Sports Image, Dale's souvenir business, manufactured 9,153 T-shirts proclaiming "On The Pole At The Glen . . . It Hurts So Good." The shirts were flown to Binghamton, New York, and picked up Friday night at 11:15 P.M. By 7:00 A.M. the next morning, they were for sale at the track's souvenir trailers. Before the Watkins Glen race began, the shirts were completely sold out. In less than twenty-four hours, Dale Earnhardt Incorporated earned $183,000 in special edition sales.

Even without such dramatic events, Earnhardt's earnings are impressive. During a Winston Cup event, the Earnhardt trailers sell approximately 5,000 T-shirts per day. At $20 a shirt, that is $100,000 per day. For a three-day weekend, T-shirt sales gross approximately $250,000.[7] Now multiply this by thirty-two Winston Cup events. Then add in all the T-shirts sold at other outlets away from the track, plus all the baseball caps, jackets, golf shirts, baby clothes, and towels.

So how much is Dale Earnhardt's souvenir business worth? Action Performance, a distributor of motorsports collectibles and consumer products, put the value at $30 million. That is how much they paid

Earnhardt, in 1996, for his company, Sports Image, Incorporated. Sports Image, with seventy employees, was organized in the late 1980s to manage and distribute Dale Earnhardt souvenirs through a network of wholesale distributors and trackside event trailers. Annual sales were in the $40 million to $50 million range before Action Performance purchased the company; Earnhardt, savvy businessman that he is, still receives royalties from each and every sale.

It is also interesting to consider how NASCAR's souvenir numbers compare with other sports. According to Doug Rose, marketing director at the West Chester, Pennsylvania–based QVC Network, "In the sports category, NASCAR's total sales are second only to the NFL."[8] Currently, NASCAR souvenir sales is the fastest-growing segment within QVC; its growth rate beats that of the overall company. What also impresses QVC is that NASCAR sales are tops in "dollars sold per minute." At QVC, you can increase sales simply by devoting more air time to a product. But the standout products don't need more air time to sell, explains Rose.

QVC has become so impressed with NASCAR that it now produces a segment devoted exclusively to racing. "Race Fans Only" is one of the company's more popular programs. On June 4, 1996, QVC produced a Michael Jordan two-hour souvenir program; gross sales totaled $726,819. The night before, Dale Earnhardt souvenirs, over the same two-hour period, grossed $741,266.[9]

In 1997, Action Performance continued its investment in NASCAR by purchasing Motorsports Traditions Limited, a distribution company, for $7 million and 57,000 shares of Action stock. Motorsports Traditions, based in Concord, North Carolina, generates approximately $25 million in annual sales, distributing and marketing apparel and souvenir items for Terry Labonte, Jeff Gordon, Ricky Craven, Darrell Waltrip, Michael Waltrip, Bobby Labonte, Jimmy Spencer, and Johnny Benson.

Although Action Performance bought the distribution business of both Sports Image and Motorsports Traditions, the drivers, Dale Earnhardt included, continue to receive royalties from their souvenir sales. In addition, NASCAR itself earns millions each year in souvenir sales.

The Collectibles Market

Apart from the many popular consumer items such as T-shirts, baseball caps, keychains, mugs, and coolers, another lucrative business, the NASCAR collectible market, is every bit as dynamic as for baseball, football, and basketball collectibles.

There is no set guideline that differentiates a souvenir from a collectible. What is collectible is defined by the collector. Generally speaking, souvenir items are mass merchandise of lower quality that rarely appeal to collectors. Collectibles are high-quality items produced in limited quantities. The market is an exquisitely simple demonstration of the law of supply and demand. For example, a Dale Earnhardt Winchester 94 .30-.30 rifle, of which 1,000 were produced, originally sold for $1,395. Today, that rifle sells for $3,000. A limited edition Richard Petty Smith & Wesson .45-caliber revolver originally sold for $495. Collectors are now swapping that revolver for $5,000.

Racing collectibles are a serious market. The Racing Collectibles Club of America, a division of Action Performance, claims 75,000 registered members; its quarterly newsletter, *RCCA News*, keeps club members up to date on the market. There are also two magazines devoted to the collectible market: *Becket Racing Monthly* and *RPM—Racing*Prices*Memorabilia*. Each magazine includes brief articles about the market and then thirty pages of recent prices paid by collectors. If you have a 1994 Action Pack 24k Gold trading card of Jeff Gordon (#189G), for example, according to *Becket*, it's worth $350.

Trading cards are popular collector items in all sports, NASCAR included. But the most popular collectible for race fans is die-cast cars. In fact, die-cast cars have become a separate hobby within the collectible market. According to *RCCA News*, approximately 2,500 club members purchase these model cars each month.

Die-cast cars are exact replicas of the race cars, trucks, and transporters for all Winston Cup teams. They are painted identical to their racing counterparts, including sponsorship decals. The die-cast market is dominated by three manufacturers, Action Performance, Revell, and Racing Champions. All have earned a reputation for producing high-quality models, and all have learned that the value of their product increases relative to a limited supply. Production runs are generally between 5,000 and 10,000 cars.

The models are manufactured in two sizes: 1:64 scale and 1:24 scale. The smaller cars retail for approximately $9, the larger ones for $35. A 1:64 model car costs approximately $0.50 to manufacture and wholesales for $4.50; the driver receives between $0.40 and $0.50 per car. The larger model costs about $9 to manufacture and wholesales for $22; the driver gets $2 per car. Thus, for a 10,000-car production run, a driver might earn $25,000—$5,000 for the small version and $20,000 for the larger version.

Although there is interest in keeping supply tight, a 10,000-car production run is not necessarily the limit for one year. If the model is selling briskly, another production can be ordered. Still another way to increase sales is to bring out model versions of special promotional cars. In real size, Jeff Gordon's Jurassic Park car, dinosaurs and all, is a promotion for Universal Studios; a model of it becomes a special collectible item.

NASCAR drivers work hard for their money. Sponsors who underwrite the teams require the drivers to make a set number of appearances each year; and the teams, remember, have more than one sponsor. Companies that pay the drivers handsomely for personal endorsements exact their time commitments as well. There are constant requests for appearances at charity events. Filming for a television commercial can take days.

The drivers have one day off a week: Monday. Tuesday through Thursday are filled with public appearances, autograph signings, speaking engagements, media interviews, and more. The pace is demanding, the stress level intense. Friday, Saturday, and Sunday are spent at the track, where a different kind of pressure takes over. The season is long, from February into December; most of January is taken up with test sessions. With luck, drivers get about three weeks of vacation.

Through it all, they must work to stay in good physical shape. Driving a race car is no picnic. It takes stamina, fast reflexes, and great physical strength; courage is assumed. Jeff Gordon does 500 pushups a day, not because he likes to but because he knows he needs the upper-body strength to wrestle the power of 700 horses for four straight hours.

Race Fans

No other sport relies so much on its fans for success as NASCAR. All sports make grateful reference to the fans, in varying degrees of sincerity, and within each sport there are a few fans who qualify as fanatics. But no sport matches the unique relationship that exists in NASCAR between athletes and fans, or the depth of loyalty the fans feel. In NASCAR, you are either a passionate fan or not a fan at all. Indifference is not a category.

The plain truth is, NASCAR fans are the financial underpinning for the sport. By purchasing tickets at full prices for every available seat, the fans financially support the track owner. By buying T-shirts, caps, and die-cast cars, the fans financially support the drivers. By consciously purchasing the products and services of sponsors, NASCAR fans help support race teams. If the race fans didn't attend events, didn't buy souvenirs or a sponsor's products, the sport would wobble like a two-legged stool.

Compare this to the other major sports. Baseball parks, generally, don't sell out their seats, basketball players receive little compensation from souvenir sales, and football fans are largely indifferent to their sport's sponsorship products. So where does the money come from to keep these sports viable? The answer is television. Without the billion-dollar television contracts, baseball, basketball, and football would implode.

Television rights, as we have learned, are becoming an increasingly important financial ingredient for NASCAR, particularly for track owners. But NASCAR, financially speaking, has done outstandingly well without them. This is a sport that was born, raised, and prospered on the interlocking support of its fans.

In the Huddle

NASCAR has long promoted itself as the only sport that allows its fans into the locker room. Around the garage area and pit row, hundreds of race fans, most of them guests of the major sponsors, are given special tours. They walk among the NASCAR officials, race crews, and drivers. They stare at the giant eighteen-wheel transporters and click pictures of the race cars beginning to line up on pit row. The corporate entertainment advantage that NASCAR has over football, baseball, and basketball is clearly visible. At a football game, you may be a special guest and sit in a corporate suite, but you won't get a tour of the sidelines and you won't get to walk among the players.

Joe Gibbs understands the value of this accessibility as well as anyone in sports. He spent years in the National Football League as coach of the Washington Redskins before joining NASCAR as a team owner. "What NASCAR has done is better than the NFL, better than almost any other sport," he said. "If you [a fan] were at a NFL game, and you'd get within 20 yards of Troy Aikman, you get arrested. These guys [NASCAR fans] can walk right up to Dale Earnhardt or Bobby Labonte."[10]

Of course, it is impossible to give all 150,000 fans at a racetrack a guided tour of the garage area. Even so, NASCAR offers its fans an opportunity that other fans can only dream about. With radio electronics and a headset, NASCAR fans can listen to the communications between the crew and the driver. It is like being in the huddle.

Since the early 1970s, two-way radio communications have been standard equipment for race teams. In the past few years, more and more race fans have begun to purchase scanners that permit them to listen to all the action. It is the same technology that allows citizens to listen to fire department and police communications.

For as little as $250, you can purchase a 100-channel automatic scanner that allows you to listen in on every race team. If you want to listen to the officiating, NASCAR officials operate on four channels. If you want to check into the big picture, you can use your scanner to listen to the MRN radio broadcast. If you come to the race without a scanner, don't despair. Many souvenir trailers sell scanners and a list of all the team frequencies. And if you can't attend a race, there is still a way to hear the action. FanScan Access Cards allow race fans to listen to their favorite teams by telephone. For $15, fans get ten minutes of access time to the network used for the scanning radios at the track.

Clubs, Camps, and Camaraderie

To complete the picture, it is important to understand that NASCAR's relationship with its fans extends beyond the racetrack.

Every NASCAR Winston Cup driver and many Busch Grand National drivers organize fan clubs. For $10, you can join Ricky Craven's fan club. Craven drives the No. 25 Budweiser Monte Carlo for Hendrick Motorsports. As a member of his fan club, you get a personalized 8" × 10" photo, a membership card and certificate, and a bumper sticker. You also get discounts on sponsorship-related souvenirs. For the latest information about Craven, you can check out his own Web page at www.rickycraven.com.

If you can't reach your driver for an autograph at the race, you can always send the item you want autographed to the fan club; it will be promptly signed and returned. Many drivers send newsletters to their fans, filled with information about the driver, his team, and the racing season. Several drivers go one step further and host open houses for the fans. Dale Earnhardt, Rusty Wallace, and Bill Elliott host club meetings each year, where they sign autographs and chat with their loyal fans.

Bill Elliott, who drives the No. 94 McDonald's Ford Thunderbird, has been voted NASCAR's most popular stock car driver in eleven different years. Elliott's fan club meetings, held at his race shop after the season's final race at Atlanta, attract 5,000 people. Many of them wait in line for six hours to get a chance to say hello to their favorite driver and tour his race shop and museum. The McDonald's pit crew puts on several demonstrations for the fans, while youngsters race pedal-powered McDonald's stock cars around the parking lot. In 1996, Jason and Diane Castle traveled from Connecticut to Dawsonville, Georgia, to attend the Bill Elliott Fan Club Appreciation Day. While there, the couple was married with both Bill Elliott and his wife, Cindy, in attendance.

Some die-hard fans want still more, and there are avenues that allow them to get even closer. Baseball has its fantasy camps; NASCAR fans have racing schools.

There are several high-performance driving schools across the country, but two of the more popular courses that focus on NASCAR-style driving are Buck Baker's Racing School and the Richard Petty Driving Experience. Both schools offer one-day courses for beginners and three-day courses for the more intense fans. Both schools conduct courses at several different tracks, including Charlotte, Atlanta, Richmond, Orlando, and Las Vegas. Over 5,500 people passed through the Petty School in 1996. The costs range from a few hundred dollars to several thousand dollars, depending on the experience.

If driving race cars over 100 mph goes further into the NASCAR experience than you want to go, there are still other opportunities to get close to the sport. One of the most popular is the annual Winston Cup Preview held every year in Winston-Salem, North Carolina. In 1997, 18,000 fans showed up to meet their favorite drivers and to view the new paint schemes for the race cars. There is an auction of racing memorabilia and plenty of autographs. Proceeds from the preview benefited Brenner Children's Hospital AirCare and the Winston Cup Racing Wives Auxiliary.

In every way, NASCAR works to heighten the experience for its fans. By doing so, it continues to strengthen the bond that exists between the fans and the sport, thereby guaranteeing its future success. I am constantly amazed at the level of commitment NASCAR fans have for this sport. After the 1996 Pocono Raceway Winston Cup event, fans endured hours of traffic jams before they were able to reach Interstate 81. Then, after just a few miles on the Interstate, they began pulling over at rest stops, offramps, and overhead passes. They all got out of their cars and gathered in clusters by the side of the road, and waited.

A few hours later, the race team transporters, carrying the race cars and equipment, also began heading home on Interstate 81. As they passed by, the fans came alive, waving banners and cheering. The transporters blasted their horns and flashed their lights in response. I can't think of another sport where watching the athletes move from one place to another is an event in itself, but, among NASCAR fans, "truck watching" has become part of the day's experience.

American Heroes

What is it about NASCAR that creates so many passionate fans who willingly spend so much money on this sport? What does stock car racing have that baseball, basketball, and football lack?

There is much about NASCAR racing that draws people to it. For one thing, it is easy to identify with the activity. Almost every adult in America knows how to drive a car, and most can remember the teenage thrill of driving *fast*. Many fans own cars that, except for the paint job, look just like the cars on the racetrack. Unlike other sports, you don't have to be a certain size, weight, or height to be a race driver. So it's not too much of a stretch for fans to imagine themselves behind the wheel of those powerful cars.

Something in the human psyche is attracted to danger, and that too is part of the appeal. Today's race cars are many times safer than ordinary passenger vehicles; nonetheless, there is always the sense that something spectacular could happen at any moment. Finally, racing is inherently exciting in a way that many other sports are not. The noise, the vibration, the speed all combine to affect observers in a powerful, almost visceral way.

All those factors, however, would not be enough to explain the loyalty of the NASCAR fans were it not for one other critical ingredient: the intense emotional bond that exists between fans and their drivers. That bond rests on a foundation of courtesy, humility, and respect that runs both ways. The drivers' attitude toward their fans is the unique factor that sets NASCAR apart and makes its drivers genuine heroes.

The association between athlete and hero is very common in this country. Championship football, basketball, and baseball players are elevated to a higher level. The best athletes become role models whether they choose to or not. Kids hang posters and wear jerseys of their favorite athlete. In their minds, these heroes can do no wrong.

But over the past several years, many fans have come to question the notion of athlete as hero. Not only has illegal behavior, including drug usage and sexual misconduct, turned fans off, but they see a common attitude of aloofness. The general perception is that today's sports superstars have no time for their fans, not even a casual acknowledgment. NASCAR's athletes, the drivers, are built differently.

Many professional athletes bring hostility to their sport; NASCAR drivers bring humility. Many professional athletes talk about their own accomplishments and tend to use "I"; NASCAR athletes talk about their team's accomplishments and mostly use "we." Many professional athletes argue and hold out for more money; NASCAR drivers will do almost anything to get a ride with a race team. Many professional athletes look for guarantees; NASCAR drivers seek opportunities. Many professional athletes ignore their fans, but NASCAR drivers embrace them all. In spite of the many demands and pressures that might pull them in the opposite direction, all the drivers willingly make time for their fans. Even when it's not convenient, they still stop to sign autographs, pose for pictures, shake a hand, hug a kid.

NASCAR is fortunate that its first superstar, Richard Petty, set the tone for all other participants. "The people who come to see me race pay to get in," Petty once said. "If they didn't come, there would be no racing and hence there would be no Richard Petty. The very least that I can do in return is be nice and receptive to them and spend time with them, whether they root for me or against me."[11]

Be nice to your fans and they will support you and the sport. This simple concept has been all but forgotten in most of the sports world. Reporters who cover other sports frequently comment, with amazement, on the level of accessibility they observe in NASCAR. Race fans and drivers consider it normal. They wouldn't have it any other way.

The NASCAR Family

In addition to the bond that links fans and drivers, another connection unites the membership within this sport. It is called the NASCAR family. The passionate race fan provides the loyalty and financial support that keep this business going, but the NASCAR family provides the moral support for those things that money can't provide.

The NASCAR family encompasses two different units: the traditional family unit of drivers and crews with their wives and children, and the larger NASCAR family.

Because race teams spend so much time away from home, it is not unusual for family members to gather at a race for the weekend. This is particularly true for drivers, whose schedule of personal appearances requires travel during the week, in addition to time at the track on the weekend. If the driver's family did not attend races, there would be little time left to see each other.

At all events, track operators cordon off an area for drivers' recreational vehicles. The RVs become a temporary home for drivers and their families. The drivers' area looks very much like a camp-ground, with barbecues, kids' toys, and baby swimming pools. For all the years their fathers are involved in racing, many children spend every weekend at a racetrack. One reason there are so many father–son combinations in NASCAR is that kids grow up in the sport.

Families are very much a part of the prerace festivities. It is not uncommon to see drivers being interviewed while holding their smallest children in their arms. After the morning NASCAR meeting, many drivers and their wives and children attend church at the track. The Motor Racing Outreach (MRO) program holds a church service each Sunday for all NASCAR members. In the afternoon, while their dads are racing around the track, children may attend the MRO Sunday School in a neighboring RV.

NASCAR has always supported a family-style environment for drivers; it is very much a part of the sport's heritage. Because a family, the France family, started the NASCAR organization and helped build the sport, the concept of family support is central to NASCAR.

The reason the system works so well is that, in addition to each family unit being accepted within the sport, all of the family units are embraced in the larger NASCAR family. It is an extended relationship that reaches out to include every member and every member's family.

Being a part of the NASCAR family is very much like being in a fraternity or a clan. NASCAR wives share and support each other; their children become fast friends. During a race, drivers are fierce competitors, but in the garage area they often joke and swap stories with each other. Likewise, crew members from different teams are often seen talking together and laughing. If a team is struggling, it is not unusual to see competing teams sharing some helpful advice. They know the favor will be returned.

It is hard not to get caught up in the Americanism of stock car racing. Each race is its own Fourth of July, with barbecues, horseshoes, kids playing, flags flying, and anthems being sung. Drivers walk to their cars from the RV area, holding hands with their wives, their children bouncing along behind. One last hug for the kids, and they're ready to go. Just before strapping in, they turn and wave to the race fans; the crowd roars.

Whatever they may have done to prepare themselves mentally for the race—and all drivers do it differently—once in the car they become very, very quiet. Their eyes focus off somewhere in the distance, and each man makes his own kind of prayer. Now, after all the hard work that all the team members have done, it all comes down to him.

Dale Earnhardt gets up every day at 5:00 A.M. Even with seventy victories and seven Winston Cup Championships, the competitive fire burns deep inside him. At forty-six, Earnhardt shows no sign of slowing down. The victories don't come as easy today, but there is no one who believes he has lost the ability to drive a race car on the edge.

By all accounts, Dale Earnhardt has become not only one of the most successful drivers in NASCAR but also one of its most successful businessmen. Even after selling Sports Image to Action Performance, Dale Earnhardt Incorporated today employs over seventy people. Three secretaries help keep him organized, and four full-time pilots make sure he reaches all of his appointments. He owns a working farm with 200 head of cattle and 32,000 chickens, not to mention a Chevrolet dealership and three race teams.

Teresa, Dale's wife, owns the No. 16 team in the NASCAR Craftsman Truck series, driven by Ron Hornaday, Jr.—the 1996 Champion. Dale and Teresa also own the No. 3 team in the NASCAR Busch Grand National series, driven by a talented rookie,

Steve Park. Recently, they have started building a new Winston Cup team that will likely compete full time in 1998. To house these race teams, the Earnhardts built a state-of-the-art 104,000-square-foot race shop and museum. For the teams, they employ mechanics, fabricators, and pit crews; they also provide eighteen-wheel transporters and the latest in racing equipment.

Dale Earnhardt has everything a driver needs to compete in Winston Cup racing, but he does not drive for his own team. Earnhardt has decided to stay with Richard Childress Racing through the year 2000, for one reason: If he wins one more Winston Cup championship, he will top Richard Petty's record. So he has chosen to stay with one of NASCAR's top race teams.

Success in NASCAR racing takes more than outstanding driving skill. Even the greatest drivers win only when they are driving the best cars built by the best race teams. The celebrity that has made Earnhardt rich is due as much to the race team as to his own ability to drive race cars, and he knows it.

7

FORTY-TWO TEAMS
ON THE SAME FIELD
AT THE SAME TIME

TIM FLOCK STARED out at the beach, his face reflecting his disappointment. The year before, he had won the 1954 Daytona Beach and Road Course right here on this very beach, only to be disqualified over a minor rule violation. Disgusted, Flock, a former Grand National Champion, quit NASCAR and returned to Atlanta to run a Pure Oil service station. But here he was, a year later, back at Daytona and itching to race again—except this time he was without a car or a team.

Flock had not planned to return to racing. However, when his buddy, Fred Wilson, stopped by the service station to invite him to go down to Daytona and watch the race, Flock didn't have to be asked twice.

Watching the practice runs at Daytona, Flock glanced around and noticed a brand-new Chrysler 300 parked on the beach. Elbowing

159

Wilson in the side, Flock said, "Boy, if I had that car, I could win this race again this year."

A man standing in front of Flock turned around and asked, "Well, just who are you?"

"I'm Tim Flock and I won this race last year."

The man smiled, extended his hand, and said, "Hello, Tim. My name is Tommy Hagood. I know the man who owns that car, and I know he hasn't got a driver for it yet."[1]

Flock couldn't believe his good luck. A week ago, he was in Atlanta pumping gas, and now he was in Daytona looking over this big beautiful Chrysler primed for the Beach race but with no driver.

Hagood gave Flock a rundown on the situation. The car's owner was Carl Kiekhafer, a millionaire from Fond du Lac, Wisconsin. Kiekhafer owned the Mercury Outboard Motor Company and he had come to NASCAR for one purpose: to promote his product. His market research showed that NASCAR fans also had an interest in motorboats, so Kiekhafer reasoned that a race car with Mercury Outboards painted across the side would be good advertising.

Hagood offered to introduce Flock to Kiekhafer, so the two drove out to an abandoned airstrip where Kiekhafer was testing some cars. Already Flock was impressed; nobody in NASCAR was conducting in-depth tests, much less renting entire airports to do so. Kiekhafer and Flock hit it off, and the next morning Flock was up early testing the Chrysler 300 while a team of mechanics measured results. Kiekhafer was serious about winning the Daytona Beach race.

Fireball Roberts, driving a Buick, won the 1955 Daytona Beach and Road Course race. Flock came in second. But when a postrace inspection discovered that the push rods on Fireball's car had been altered, he was disqualified and the race was awarded to Flock. In one bold stroke, Kiekhafer burst into NASCAR, fielded a winning race team, and increased his marketing prowess.

If one winning NASCAR team was good, Kiekhafer figured, then several teams would be even better. With multiple entries, he would stand a better chance at winning more races and increasing his company's exposure. So he hired Tim Flock's brothers, the old moonshine runners Fonty and Bob, to drive cars for him, and then he added Speedy Thompson, another talented NASCAR driver.

To no one's surprise, Tim Flock and Kiekhafer won the 1955 Grand National Championship. When the 1956 season started, Kiekhafer brought two more Chryslers to Daytona, adding drivers Frank Mundy and Buck Baker. Now Kiekhafer had six cars, six drivers. It was the first multicar team in NASCAR, and it was immensely successful. In the first twenty-five races of the 1956 season, Kiekhafer's drivers won twenty-one times, including an unprecedented sixteen races in a row.

"Kiekhafer was decades ahead of his time," observes Humpy Wheeler, current president of Charlotte Motor Speedway. "He introduced a number of innovations that changed the sport in a better way."[2] Kiekhafer was meticulous and left nothing to chance. He constantly tested his cars, checking tires, air pressure, and wheel sizes. He would alter the setting on carburetors and gear ratios and test again, carefully recording and analyzing the results. How the car was set up for each race was recorded in minute detail, so the next time the car appeared at the track, there was a trail of information. Kiekhafer even employed a full-time meteorologist as a consultant to the team about weather conditions.

Kiekhafer was also a generous man. He flew team members and their families to races in his company plane. He awarded his drivers 100 percent of the prize winnings and paid them bonuses for special appearances. Kiekhafer was interested only in publicity for Mercury Outboard Motors. The crew and drivers were outfitted in identical crisp white uniforms and, on race day, Kiekhafer transported his race team to the track in enclosed car haulers. "It was a sight to see those big beautiful white transport trucks come streaming into the track," remembers Paul Sawyer, president of Richmond International Raceway.[3]

But although he was generous, Kiekhafer was also a hard taskmaster. With each victory, he demanded more and more from the team. Tension among crew members, drivers, and Kiekhafer was high. Tim Flock left in midseason with stomach ulcers and was replaced with Herb Thomas, an equally gifted driver. Shortly after joining the Kiekhafer team, Thomas quit as well.

Although the Mercury Outboard team continued to win races, it seemed very few enjoyed the ride. Even the fans grew tired of seeing Kiekhafer's cars win every race. At some point during the season, fan cheers turned to boos. Finally, when sales of Mercury Outboard motors began to suffer, Kiekhafer decided to shut down the racing operation at the end of the season. Buck Baker won the 1956 Grand National, and Kiekhafer, with back-to-back championships, went home to Wisconsin, never to race again. It would be forty years before another team owner successfully implemented a multicar strategy.

The Makeup of a NASCAR Team

To compete at the highest level in NASCAR Winston Cup racing requires a fast car, a capable driver, and a responsive crew. It may be the driver who gets all the media attention, but make no mistake, a platoon of people behind each driver makes winning possible.

Putting these pieces together is the responsibility of a team owner. From his own resources, like Carl Kiekhafer, or with the help of sponsorship dollars, like most owners today, the team owner bears all the financial risk of putting a team in competition. This includes hiring a driver and then acquiring all the necessary equipment and personnel to build a race car, test the car, transport the car to the track, and then support the car and the driver during the race.

The easiest way to understand a team's structure is to mentally divide the team into three divisions: (1) administrative, (2) shop operations, and (3) race-day operations.

The administrative functions are largely back-office support positions, including secretarial, clerical, and accounting. Included in this category is one of the team's most important jobs: team manager. Next to the owner, the team manager carries the greatest overall responsibility for the team. The manager oversees the day-to-day operations, including managing the administrative office, paying bills, deciding personnel issues, supervising travel arrangements, entertaining guests and sponsors at race events, and serving as the primary liaison with NASCAR. As the sport has grown, some teams have added public relations managers who do nothing but coordinate the needs of their guests and sponsors. This includes arranging show cars and appearances of their team's driver, and supplying reporters with information about the team. If they do not have a public relations person on staff, many teams contract the services of an outside PR agency.

The responsibility of managing the race shop operations falls to the crew chief. In all matters relating to the technical aspects of the car, including building it in the shop and monitoring how it performs at the track, the decisions rest with the crew chief. The crew chief hires the race shop personnel, including a shop foreman, engine builders, fabricators, machinists, engineers, mechanics, gear/transmission specialists, a parts manager, and a transport driver.

Come race day, the crew chief is still in charge—planning the race strategy, scheduling pit stops, interacting with NASCAR, managing the crew—but the spotlight shifts to the race crew. The core crew consists of seven people: front tire carrier, rear tire carrier, jackman, front tire changer, rear tire changer, gasman, and catch can man. In twenty seconds, they can change all four tires and refuel the car. In addition to these seven, a team will often bring several others for pit support during a race. Two other important team positions are the scorer, who keeps track of where the driver is throughout the race, and the spotter. Perched high above the track, the spotter stays in constant radio communication with the driver, alerting him about wrecks ahead and the positions of other race cars.

Altogether, a typical NASCAR Winston Cup team includes between twenty and thirty people. Administrative positions are largely exclusive, but many race-day personnel work in the shop during the week, helping the mechanics and engineers. On race day, the roles are reversed; shop mechanics become pit supporters. On some teams, the crew chief is also the team manager.

One thing is becoming clear. As the competition level in NASCAR continues to rise, so too will the demands on the race team. To build competitive race cars will require more automotive specialists. To consistently turn twenty-second pit stops will require the best race crews. As team owners seek more sponsorship dollars to support high-caliber personnel, sponsors in turn will require higher performance.

The Challenge of Multicar Teams

After 1956, there were other attempts to repeat what Carl Kiekhafer accomplished with his six-car team. But each time an owner put two or more drivers together, the results were friction and stress.

For all his scientific effort, Kiekhafer found only half of the formula. A multicar team needs strong financing and strong talent, which Kiekhafer willingly provided. What he could not pull off was that intangible ingredient called chemistry. No matter how great the talent or how deep the owner's pockets, unless the owner can build chemistry among all the drivers and all the crew members, a multicar operation cannot succeed.

Because of these challenges, the multicar team strategy did not fully take hold in NASCAR until the 1990s. Today, people interested in understanding that strategy eventually make their way to Papa Joe Hendrick Boulevard in Harrisburg, North Carolina, and the headquarters of Hendrick Motorsports.

Team Success

Hendrick Motorsports, owned by Rick Hendrick, is NASCAR's largest race organization. Nestled on twenty-six acres one mile west of Charlotte Motor Speedway, the Hendrick Motorsports complex comprises eight buildings, a total of 200,000 square feet. There is room for three Winston Cup teams and one Craftsman Truck team. The complex contains administrative offices, an engine shop, a chassis and fabricator shop, a research and development facility, and a gym for employees.

The Hendrick Motorsports complex also includes a 15,000-square-foot museum and souvenir shop that is open to the public free of charge. The museum showcases several Hendrick-restored race cars, including Geoff Bodine's Levi Garrett Chevrolet Lumina, Tim Richmond's Folger's Chevrolet Monte Carlo, and Darrell Waltrip's Tide Chevrolet Monte Carlo. The museum also houses racing memorabilia and countless trophies, including two

Winston Cup Championship trophies. Jeff Gordon won the 1995 championship driving the No. 24 DuPont Chevrolet Monte Carlo; in 1996, Terry Labonte won the championship driving the Kellogg's Chevrolet Monte Carlo. Thus, Rick Hendrick became the first multiteam owner since Carl Kiekhafer to win back-to-back championships with two different drivers.

Building an Empire

J. R. Hendrick III—Rick Hendrick to everyone in NASCAR—is president and CEO of Hendrick Automotive Group. With ninety automobile dealerships and over $2 billion in annual sales, Rick Hendrick is the world's largest automotive dealer, in terms of both unit sales and dollar volume. He is forty-eight years old. Although his accomplishments are impressive, his success didn't occur overnight.

Rick was family-fortunate. From his father, a tobacco farmer, he learned how to repair engines. From his mother, a bank teller, he learned how to borrow money. When Rick was fourteen, he rebuilt a 1931 Chevrolet with his father's help and set records at the local dragstrip. At sixteen, Rick was buying, repairing, and selling used cars financed with ninety-day bank notes.

For Rick Hendrick, one success led to another. He became general sales manager of a BMW/Honda/Mercedes dealership when he was twenty-three. Four years later, he borrowed enough money to buy his own Chevrolet dealership in Bennettsville, South Carolina, becoming the youngest Chevrolet dealer in the country. In the first year, Rick increased the volume of units sold at his dealership from 200 to over 1,200.

In the next ten years, Rick Hendrick expanded his automotive operations to twenty dealerships. He was selling Chevrolets, Hondas, Mercedes, Volvos, and Toyotas all across the South. Rick's teenage love affair with cars was now extended through his automobile deal-erships while his business skills were being tuned by the demands of a growing and profitable company.

Rick's official introduction to NASCAR came in 1978, when Hendrick Automotive Group purchased City Chevrolet in Charlotte. Several independent NASCAR teams that lacked De-troit manufacturer support depended on City Chevrolet for auto-motive parts. Once he owned that dealership, it was an easy jump to the decision to start a new race team a few years later. The tim-ing was fortuitous. Rick's competitive spirit and longtime love af-fair with race cars now had a natural outlet.

Smart Business Decisions

Hendrick Motorsports began in 1984 with one team and one driver: Geoff Bodine. Two years later, with the addition of driver Tim Richmond and crew chief Harry Hyde, Rick took the first step in a multicar team strategy.

For Rick, the strategy was simple and obvious. Common sense told him a two-car team would bring in twice the sponsorship dol-lars but would not necessarily require twice as much infrastructure. He would run Hendrick Motorsports like a business, pooling re-sources and manpower to take advantage of efficiencies, and build-ing a stronger presence.

"I related racing to the automobile business," Hendrick later re-called. With his automobile dealerships, Rick had learned that by "being able to share information we were more successful. I could think of no reason why the same theory wouldn't work in NASCAR."[4]

Success did not come easily. Critics argued that even with a pot full of money you couldn't buy team spirit. When famed race driver

Bobby Allison left DiGard Racing in 1985, a team with which he had won a Winston Cup Championship, because he objected to the addition of a second team, many in NASCAR said, "I told you so."

But Rick Hendrick did not give up, even though his strategy encountered some rough spots. Tim Richmond and Geoff Bodine were beginning to show promise when Tim Richmond contracted AIDS and later died. Rick responded by adding another car. Now he had a three-car team, with Geoff Bodine, Darrell Waltrip, and Ken Schrader. Before long, first Bodine and then Waltrip left to purchase their own teams. Rick quickly hired two replacement drivers: Ricky Rudd and newcomer Jeff Gordon. When Ricky Rudd left to start his own team, Hendrick hired Terry Labonte.

The Fit Factor

Some call it team spirit, others call it chemistry. At Hendrick Motorsports, it is called the Fit Factor. How well, in other words, do the pieces fit together? In this case, the pieces are human beings, and in this arena Rick Hendrick is a master.

Rick has been in sales his whole adult life. His business success at Hendrick Automotive Group is attributed to his people skills. In his early years with NASCAR, it was clear Rick knew people better than he knew racing—and that is ultimately what allowed him to succeed.

Rick Hendrick believes if you put the right people in the right positions, support them, and promote from within, your organization will strengthen. Jimmy Johnson is living proof of this concept. He began working in one of Rick's Toyota dealerships in 1983. Two years later, Rick asked Jimmy to open a new dealership in Hudson, Florida. Not long after, Johnson was asked to become general manager of the Motorsports program. Much of the financial success of

Hendrick Motorsports is attributed to the management attention of Jimmy Johnson, a Hendrick Automotive Group employee who showed promise and was promoted.

The people who race for Hendrick Motorsports freely testify to the Fit Factor. The No. 5 team is convinced. Terry Labonte will tell you, "Rick Hendrick went out and got good people, the right people and he's kept them." His crew chief, Gary DeHart, adds, "The people are what makes the difference."

Over at the No. 24 team, the attitude is the same. According to Ray Evernham, crew chief for the DuPont Chevrolet Monte Carlo, "Rick always had good equipment. It's just that now, he's got the right combination of people." Jeff Gordon, who drives the No. 24, agrees. "Rick was able to show every single person on his team that working together could pay off," he said. "They saw we can benefit from the resources that are here, and because of that, they don't mind working together."[5]

The Modern Race Shop

The days when stock cars were built in barns on dirty floors are long gone. Hendrick Motorsports is a $7 million state-of-the-art racing complex. All of the brightly lit buildings have shiny floors, and all are equipped with computers providing the latest in racing diagnostics.

The single most important decision Rick Hendrick made about his facility was to build one engine shop to be shared by all three teams. This created two important benefits: it spread the fixed costs among three teams, and it eliminated any notion that the equipment for teams was unequal. When teams feel they have to compete against one another for the best equipment, the chemistry that is so vital to success is poisoned. "The way we have it designed," says Hendrick, "there's no way you could favor one guy with an engine."

All the pistons, rods, and cylinder heads are manufactured in the same area. "When the engines get to the dynamometer there might be three to five horsepower difference, but that's it. The engines are that close."[6]

The economic benefit from shared operations is straightforward. Since he doesn't need three of everything (equipment and personnel) to build engines for three race teams, Hendrick can put the cost savings into the team. At Hendrick Motorsports, mechanics and engine builders walking the shop floor are likely to have college and postgraduate degrees in auto mechanics and aerodynamics. These specialists generate meaningful information that can be used by the engine builders and fabricators and then shared equally among the teams.

Several race teams build their own motors in-house, but Hendrick Motorsports is one of the few teams that actually build their race cars from scratch. The most important reason for in-house programs is to maintain consistency. As little as ⅜-inch difference from corner to corner on a chassis can mean differences in handling.

Hendrick Motorsports saw the value of controlling its own product from the beginning. "Basically, all of our cars are identical," says Jimmy Johnson. "There is probably five percent that the individual teams work with and customize for the way their drivers like them." About thirty Hendrick employees build the chassis. Fourteen people work on tubing and surface plates. Ten other employees wrap the steel skeleton with sheet-metal skin. Five research and development specialists work full-time figuring out how to make the cars run faster.

"The advantage of being able to do it yourself," explains Johnson, "is controlling quality. It is an assembly line but we control the assembly line."[7]

Teamwork Down the Line

Speed starts at the race shop. The motor and chassis in-house programs are constantly searching for ways to improve the cars. But even when the chassis is built, the motor installed, and the car completed, the team's work is not done; in fact, it is only beginning. The cars have to be tested, fine-tuned for qualifying runs, and maintained in perfect condition during the race itself.

Today, it is not unusual for as many as fifty teams to show up at a track, all vying for forty-two spots. Because of the pressure to qualify and because qualifying itself may depend on just tenths of a second, how well the car is made and how well it is set up become critically important. Each step in the process, from the race shop to testing to finally qualifying, requires teamwork of the highest order.

Testing

Each season, NASCAR allows a race team a maximum of seven test dates on Winston Cup tracks. The team can decide when and where it wants to test, whether it be at Charlotte, Daytona, Darlington, or Bristol. Teams use this opportunity to fine-tune their race car specifically for the track at which they are testing. Often, a team will spend time setting the car up for a fast qualifying lap and then readjust the car for longer runs under race conditions. The team is looking for the right combination that will put it ahead of competitors when it returns on race day.

NASCAR does not regulate testing at non-Winston Cup tracks. For that reason, Winston Cup teams often break in their new cars at tracks like Greenville–Pickens Speedway or Hickory Motor Speedway. You can test brakes, shock absorbers, springs, or sway bars at one of these tracks without using one of the seven valuable NASCAR test dates.

No matter where it occurs, testing is expensive. In fact, the costs are very much the same whether the team is testing or racing. In both stages, management must transport the team, buy several sets of tires, rent the track, and pay for hotel and food for the crew. Hendrick Motorsports estimates that each test costs a team approximately $150,000.

Some have suggested that organizations with a multicar team have an advantage when it comes to testing. With three race teams, NASCAR allows Hendrick Motorsports twenty-one test dates. Jimmy Johnson denies that it gives them unfair advantage. "What we have found is that each driver has his own peculiar way of driving and feeling a race car. What works for Jeff Gordon at Daytona does not necessarily work for Terry Labonte. You just can't set up both cars the same."[8]

Even the drivers have begun to question the overall value of testing. Because track conditions can vary, what worked in testing might not work on race day. Jeff Gordon points out that when track temperatures change, when there is rubber on the track, or when there are other cars driving around you, the car will handle differently. But because each race team is looking for any opportunity, however small, to gain a competitive advantage, testing will continue to absorb time, attention, and money.

Qualifying Runs

Before a team can race on Sunday, it first has to qualify on Friday. This is where the pressure on a race team begins. Because there are more race teams wanting to compete than there are available positions, some teams will inevitably fail to qualify. Corporations that pay millions of dollars to sponsor a team so their product or service can be seen by millions on race day lose their marketing opportunity if the team doesn't make it.

To qualify, each car runs one lap (sometimes two) against the clock. It is unbelievably tough. In 1986, Tim Richmond won the pole at Martinsville with a lap speed of 90.716 miles an hour. Michael Waltrip, who qualified twenty-fifth, posted a speed of 88.046 miles an hour. The difference between the two qualifiers was almost three miles an hour. Ten years later, Ricky Craven took the pole at Martinsville at 93.079. Jeff Burton qualified twenty-fifth at 92.142—a difference of less than one mile per hour.

Race Day

The advantage to a multicar team strategy is clearly demonstrated on race day. After reaping the benefits of technology and the exchange of information, after the testing and the success of qualifying, the individual drivers of the multicar team head to the track with one goal in mind: to win. Each man wants to win, but the team drivers know they can help each other.

Teamwork on the race track has become increasingly important, particularly on the superspeedways, where drafting—two or more cars racing in single file—is often the difference between winning and losing. At Hendrick Motorsports, Jeff Gordon, Terry Labonte, and Ricky Craven all maintain radio communications with their crew during a race, but they also have the opportunity to talk with each other and strategize. It is becoming common for multicar teams to hook up in a draft and then power past the single teams who are busily looking around for a drafting partner.

The 1997 Daytona 500 showed the advantage of a multicar team at its best. With five laps to go, Bill Elliott, driving the No. 94

McDonald's Ford Thunderbird, found himself sandwiched among the "Three Musketeers" of Hendrick Motorsports. Elliott, who is a single-team owner/driver, had no way to block all three Hendrick drivers. Gordon dropped down low, Labonte and Craven went high. Gordon was the first one by, and Labonte and Craven fell in line behind him, creating a draft that allowed the trio to pull away. The Hendrick Motorsports team crossed the finish line 1–2–3, and Jeff Gordon won his first Daytona 500 victory.

"I was a sitting duck at the end," Elliott commented.[9]

"Bill Elliott has seen the future of NASCAR," wrote USA Today reporter Beth Tuschak. "The winning trend in Winston Cup racing most likely lies in multicar team operations."[10]

The Crew Chief and the Pit Crew

Ray Evernham, the crew chief for the No. 24 DuPont Chevrolet team at Hendrick Motorsports, observes that great race drivers need peripheral vision, reflexes, and instincts. These are all natural abilities that, for the most part, cannot be learned. "Being a great crew chief is different," says Evernham. "I believe it is learned ability rather than just a natural thing, and that means you can do something to make yourself better."[11]

Few others have made themselves better at being a crew chief than Ray Evernham. The success of the No. 24 DuPont Chevrolet team speaks volumes. Yes, Jeff Gordon is a great race driver, but even great drivers will not succeed without a great team. Yes, Hendrick Motorsports is one of the great teams, but without a crew chief's direction, even the best driver with the best team will have difficulty winning races.

According to Ben White, a seasoned reporter for NASCAR Winston Cup Illustrated, "The one common denominator that links organizations with the word success . . . is the crew chief."[12] The reason, suggests White, is that this one person must perform multiple roles and do them all well. The crew chief organizes the race shop and its personnel. He is in charge of race day as well as the pit crew, and he becomes the lifeline connecting the driver, the car, and the track. It is an enormous responsibility, and it takes superb management skills, the ability to absorb and catalog vast amounts of information, and the guts to make tough decisions on the fly under situations of intense pressure. Some have likened the role of a crew chief on race day to that of a naval submarine commander under battle conditions.

Fortunately, today's NASCAR crew chief has as much technological assistance as submarine commanders. He records on a clipboard every bit of information about changes made in the car during practice, and the driver's comments about the car's setup. All this information is then fed into a computer and analyzed.

On race day, the computer is hooked into the pit wagon, a high-tech toolbox, and rolled down to pit row. The pit wagon contains two laptop computers, two printers, and two television monitors. One monitor is connected to a satellite dish to pick up the live broadcast of the race. The other is connected to a remote camera suspended above pit row, to tape each pit stop. One computer retrieves proprietary information (air pressure, tire wear, fuel mileage, shocks, sway bars, and so on) entered by the crew chief. The second computer links to the NASCAR computer system, which tracks lap numbers, driver positions, and weather forecasting.

All this information is instantly available and becomes the basis of a crew chief's decision. But each command in turn requires the action of the team's crew and driver. The crew chief has little control over how the driver will race the car, but he does have control over the pit crew and how well they orchestrate the twenty-second pit stop.

The difference between first and second place, in almost every single NASCAR race, is a matter of one or two seconds. And the difference between waving from victory lane and heading to the garage can frequently be found in how quickly a team executes a pit stop.

At Hendrick Motorsports, particular emphasis is placed on pit-crew performance. "Pit crews can win or lose races for you," says crew chief Ray Evernham. "So why shouldn't they receive as much attention as building a motor or a chassis?"[13]

Evernham revolutionized the concept of professional pit crew members. Each team's pit crew regularly works out in the employees' gym. To train the crew, Evernham brought in Andy Papthanassiou, a former offensive lineman at Stanford who also has a master's degree in organizational behavior. Each and every movement of each crew function was carefully choreographed, and the teams practiced relentlessly. The result: At the 30th Annual Unocal Pit Crew Championships, held at North Carolina Motor Speedway, the No. 5 Terry Labonte Kellogg's Chevrolet team took first place, followed by the No. 24 DuPont team—another 1–2 finish for Hendrick Motorsports.

Most NASCAR Winston Cup teams show up at a race with fourteen or fifteen crew members. Hendrick Motorsports brings twenty-five. There are backup crews so that if some member of a pit crew is injured or becomes sick, a trained reserve is on hand. Each NASCAR Winston Cup team has a spotter, but Ray Evernham adds spotters at each turn. He also assigns a few crew members to observe other teams in the pits and to monitor their radio communications.

The Economics of a Team

The annual budget at Hendrick Motorsports runs about $30 million. Each of the three teams costs about $7.5 million to operate, and another $7.5 million goes into team efforts such as engineering, chassis development, and fabrication.

Where does the money come from to support this operation? According to Jimmy Johnson, about 55 percent of the revenues needed comes from sponsorships. DuPont, Kellogg's, and Anheuser-Busch, the primary sponsors, pay the most; associate sponsors like Quaker State and PepsiCo kick in a little more. Royalties from the sale of merchandise and collectibles cover about 10 percent of the year's expenses (after one-third is shared with the drivers and one-third with the sponsor). Another 10 percent comes from research projects performed for General Motors.

Hendrick Motorsports is one of the few teams that leases its motors; this accounts for about 10 percent of the company's revenues. If you want a Hendrick motor for your team, you can lease one for the season or for the race, but you can't buy one. And don't even think about taking it apart to uncover its secrets. Wherever the Hendrick motor goes, a Hendrick engineer follows the motor to assist the team and prevent anyone from taking it apart.

Another 10 to 15 percent of the company's revenues comes from race winnings and other ventures, including chartering one of the team's six airplanes. In 1995, the Hendrick Motorsports team won $6.8 million; in 1996, the team won $9.3 million. Half of a race's winnings go to the driver, the other half to the organization.

The expense side of the income statement is more difficult to uncover. Teams are hesitant to show competitors where and how they are spending their money. However, we can put together some general ideas. Each race car costs between $100,000 and $150,000 to produce. Each team gets at least ten cars for the season—maybe more, if there have been several wrecks. Transporters cost $300,000 each, and travel costs for all the personnel take a big bite. But by far the greatest expense facing race teams today is the escalating salaries of its employees.

With 160 employees, including seven full-time engineers and a newly hired aerodynamicist, all of them with health coverage, retirement plans, and bonus opportunities, Hendrick Motorsports no doubt carries high payroll expenses. Crew chief salaries are approaching $300,000. Experienced fabricators and mechanics make around $50,000 each; engineers, even more.

When you drive down Papa Joe Hendrick Boulevard and turn into the Hendrick Motorsports complex, it is immediately apparent that NASCAR has outgrown the barns and outhouses. "We are challenging at the highest level of auto racing in America," said Ray Evernham. "So why shouldn't we build an organization like the Yankees or the 49ers?"[14] It may not be long before the Yankees and 49ers come down to North Carolina to learn something from Rick Hendrick.

Starting a New Winston Cup Team

The usual pathway to the Winston Cup level starts with forming a team in the NASCAR Busch Grand National series or the NASCAR Craftsman Truck series, or possibly at one of the smaller regional series. After a few years of success, teams then begin to climb up to the next level. Many of the rookie teams in NASCAR's Winston Cup were competitive teams the year before in the Busch series.

It is a far greater challenge for a rookie team to organize itself, find a sponsor, hire a driver and crew, provide the team with the latest equipment, test, and be ready for qualifying and racing at the NASCAR Winston Cup level—all within one year. This challenge is now being met by Washington Erving Motorsports.

What makes this attempt so unique is not only has this organization never competed in racing before, but it is a minority-led group run by a woman and an African American and financed by two well-known African American businessmen and former athletes. Kathy Thompson, head of Four Seasons Marketing, a Greensboro, North Carolina, NASCAR sports marketing company, will run the organization with Fields Jackson, Jr., an African American business owner from Raleigh, North Carolina. The team will be financed and owned by former NBA and NFL superstars Julius Erving ("Dr. J") and Joe Washington. It is the first minority-led and -owned NASCAR Winston Cup team since Wendell Scott. Scott, who competed in NASCAR from 1961 to 1972, is the only African American driver/owner ever to win a NASCAR race, at Jacksonville in 1964.

The genesis of Washington Erving Motorsports is an interesting story. It began with Jackson. His company, Charles Fields, is heavily involved in sports marketing at the collegiate level. The Charles Fields Company helps universities raise money by providing special commemorative artwork for alumni, students, and fans. One of the company artists, Ron Crawford, a successful African American artist in Charlotte, also works on NASCAR projects, including paintings of Jeff Gordon, Terry Labonte, Rusty Wallace, and Mark Martin. Ron also produces commemorative art such as depictions of Richard Petty's final year in NASCAR, the inaugural Brickyard stock car race in Indianapolis, and the final race at North Wilkesboro.

Joe Washington is a member of the board of directors of The Charles Fields Company. Over the past several years, the company and its board have watched the growth of NASCAR artwork outpace the company's original business in college athletics. This was no surprise to Ron Crawford, an avid NASCAR fan, or to Jackson, who relocated the company to North Carolina in order to better leverage the opportunities in racing. The biggest surprise came from the board, whose members were uneducated about NASCAR. At

Jackson's invitation, Joe Washington attended his first race in At-lanta so he could see for himself what all the excitement was about.

"I always thought stock car racing was just a bunch of guys going around in circles," Washington said. "It sounded about as exciting as watching paint dry."[15] But by the time the race started, Washington was convinced. The people, the color, the noise, the vibration, the speed, the action—all combined to create a level of excitement in Joe Washington that he didn't expect. It was something he had not felt since his days in football. The crowning touch came when Kathy Thompson, a friend of Jackson, arranged a meeting at the track be-tween Joe Washington and Joe Gibbs.

Joe Gibbs, former coach of the Washington Redskins, and Joe Washington, a former Redskins running back, had shared many ex-citing moments in their careers, including winning the 1982 Super Bowl. When they met at the Atlanta Motor Speedway, the reunion was emotional. After the hugs and back slapping, Washington began to quiz his former coach about racing. "Coach Gibbs was phenome-nal," said Washington. "He laid out the good and bad about the sport. I knew if Coach Gibbs left football for racing, it said a lot about the sport."

Joe Gibbs is the owner of the No. 18 Interstate Batteries Pontiac Grand Prix team. His driver, Bobby Labonte, the brother of Terry Labonte, has been making steady progress over the past two years, winning poles and races.

Gibbs sees NASCAR as opportunity. At their meeting in Atlanta, Gibbs told Jackson that NASCAR today reminded him of where pro-fessional football was in the early years. There was still so much to accomplish in NASCAR, Gibbs argued, with the possibility of new teams and new tracks in new markets. "This sport needs you," Gibbs told Washington, "and I'll help you." That was the clincher.

"Once you have competed in professional sports, there are very few things that can restore the basic challenge in life," said Washington. Now, with NASCAR, he had been given a challenge he could not turn down: to become the first minority-owned Winston Cup team to compete and win in modern times.

The first thing Washington did when he returned home from Atlanta was call his friend, Julius Erving. Both men, whose families had become close over the years, had been looking for a business opportunity they could share. "But Julius had no interest in NASCAR," Washington recounted. "His reaction to stock car racing was the same as mine." The only way to convince him was to take him to a race. Reluctantly, Julius agreed.

"By the time the race started at Daytona and Julius looked out at the 150,000 screaming fans and race cars storming by at 180 miles an hour with Fortune 500 sponsorships pasted everywhere, I could tell his interest was up," Washington remembered. Then Washington put Julius and Coach Gibbs together and sat back and waited. After the meeting, Erving and Gibbs shook hands. "I could see his smile," said Washington, "and I knew he was convinced."

When Joe Washington and Julius Erving stood before reporters on May 21, 1997, and announced they were forming a new Winston Cup team and a Busch series team and that both would begin racing in 1998, more than a few were skeptical. The 1998 Daytona 500, the season opener, was less than nine months away. Wendell Scott's family attended the press conference. Wendell, the first African American NASCAR winner, had passed away in 1990, but his wife Mary and his daughter Sybil were there. Said Sybil, "I must believe that he's smiling on this announcement and that he is pleased that he's being recognized as the gentleman who broke a barrier that had to come down."[16]

But despite the skepticism, most came away with the idea that if anyone could pull this off, it was Joe Washington and Julius Erving. "We are used to winning," said Jackson, "and the last thing we want to do is have our team run into walls and fail to qualify for races." Joe Gibbs has agreed to advise Washington Erving Motorsports; Ford Motor Company will provide parts, technical support, and marketing expertise.

There are two ways to start a NASCAR Winston Cup team. You can buy a team from another owner or start one from scratch and build your own. Driver Brett Bodine started his own team by buying the racing operations, including cars and equipment, from his owner, Junior Johnson, for $5 million. It seemed to be a fair price. Most people agree you can start a Winston Cup team and put it into competition for about $4 million or $5 million a year; a Busch team costs about $2 million. The Washington Erving Motorsports annual operating budget is $6 million.

The team owners will begin by leasing a race shop until they are ready to build their own complex. They will purchase eight chassis for $15,000 each, and will prepare two cars for four different types of tracks: short track, speedway, superspeedway, and road course. Until the team can develop its own motor program, team owners will lease engines in the first year for a cost of between $1 million and $1.3 million. They will buy a transporter and hire employees—general manager, crew chief, shop mechanics, pit crew, and, of course, a driver.

The money spent will be offset by sponsorship dollars. What Washington and Erving lack in racing experience they more than make up for in business contacts and corporate invitations. They believe the racing operation will break even in the first two years. The crossover will come from the countless merchandising opportunities that both Washington and Erving expect to gain.

Washington and Erving are dead serious; they want their team to be competitive from the start, so that one day there will be another minority driver on the level of Wendell Scott. "Obviously having a minority crew chief or minority driver right now would be great; but we're also realistic about this," said Washington. "We hope to create a program where we can solicit minority drivers. One thing that we don't want to do is to omit any prospective driver of any race, creed, or color."[17]

The Silly Season

In NASCAR, changing jobs is an annual event. It affects only a small number of people in a sport with over 50,000 members, but it produces a large swarm of rumors. Inside the garages, people begin to speculate about which driver is going to leave which team to join another. What crew chief is being courted to take over a struggling operation? It is called the "silly season" and it happens in NASCAR every year.

To a degree, the silly season is made sillier by NASCAR's particular version of the chicken-and-egg dilemma. Few drivers will sign on to a team until they know who the sponsor will be, but few sponsors will write checks until they know who their driver will be. Because of this dilemma, formal announcements of change are usually delayed until the season's end, but the rumor mill kicks into high gear much earlier, typically in the second half of the year.

By midpoint in any season, half of the race teams may have something to cheer about while the other half are looking for reasons why they have performed so badly. Silly season affects both the poor-performance teams and the strong performers. On poor-performance teams, owners, crew members, crew chiefs, and drivers all look at the operation closely, trying to find the weak link. Everyone knows that something on the team is out of sync and that a shakeup in the organization is needed. Often, the driver is on the hot seat. As with any other sport, if you're not winning, your job is at risk.

Drivers are not likely to leave successful programs, but successful crew chiefs and crew members are often courted by other teams, in the hope that their magic can work on a troubled organization.

If you were to ask race team members considering a change what type of organization they are looking for, their answer is rather obvious. They would like to join a team where salaries are competitive, where the opportunities for advancement are plentiful, and where a winning attitude is commonplace. In other words, at Hendrick Motorsports. Or someplace just like it.

In NASCAR's first fifty years, Carl Kiekhafer, even with his brief tenure, is considered to be one of the sport's most successful team owners. But Kiekhafer left behind only half the answer to the puzzle of what it takes to succeed. Rick Hendrick has figured out the other half. By coupling a financially strong multicar organization with strong team chemistry, Hendrick Motorsports has apparently become the team model for NASCAR's next fifty years.

Dark Clouds on a Sunny Horizon

I did not know what to expect. My wife and I were sitting in the Grand Ballroom of the Waldorf-Astoria Hotel in New York City, just minutes before the start of the NASCAR Winston Cup Awards Banquet. The banquet is the festive close to the Winston Cup season, and practically everyone in NASCAR was there. The room was buzzing with talk and laughter, but the excitement was muted. There was plenty of happiness for Terry Labonte, the 1996

NASCAR Winston Cup Champion, but it was being overshadowed by an announcement just two days earlier.

A federal grand jury in Asheville, North Carolina, had indicted Rick Hendrick on charges of conspiring to bribe Honda executives in order to receive preferential treatment in the allocation of Honda automobiles. The federal government had been investigating the possibility of corruption for over two years, and Hendrick had cooperated with investigators. Whatever the turn of events, the timing of the announcement, just two days before the Winston Cup banquet, was seen by all as a blatant attempt to purposely embarrass Rick Hendrick.

It is customary to place the head table of the winning team on the stage of the ballroom; the winning driver, crew chief, and team owner, with their wives, are seated at this elevated table. Rick's introduction would be first.

As the moment approached, the anticipation of what was going to happen became almost uncomfortable. The lights were dimmed, the room grew quiet, and the spotlight hit center stage. The master of ceremonies moved to the microphone, paused, and then introduced the owner of the 1996 NASCAR Winston Cup Championship team, Rick Hendrick.

The room exploded. People jumped to their feet, clapping and cheering as Rick and his wife Linda stepped on stage. The ovation continued while the Hendricks, hand in hand, made their way to the head table. The cheering was so loud that Rick had to stop midway. Linda let go of his hand and stepped slightly back; slowly, Rick Hendrick bowed to his friends and colleagues. The crowd responded with even louder cheering.

Overall, the evening was a roaring success. Driver Terry Labonte received his second NASCAR Winston Cup Championship; owner Rick Hendrick received his second in a row. Rick looked tired and drained, but considering what had happened earlier in the week, that was to be expected. No one except Rick and Linda knew the other secret. Weeks earlier, Rick Hendrick had been diagnosed with a rare form of leukemia. Already his physical stamina was being tested.

As I planned the writing of this chapter, I was worried that the announcement of Rick Hendrick's illness and legal woes would distract readers from understanding and appreciating the success at Hendrick Motorsports. It has become, after all, the model many team owners, including Richard Childress, Robert Yates, Felix Sabates, Jack Roush, and Joe Gibbs, are now trying to replicate.

But we must all take note: Whatever the ultimate outcome, Rick Hendrick's challenges have worked to further illustrate the bond and strength of the NASCAR family, the backbone that holds this sport together.

Shortly after the grand jury indictment, Bill France, Jr. issued a statement; "When it comes to motorsports, we wish we had more car owners like Mr. Hendrick. The results of Hendrick Motorsports on the racetrack speak for themselves. Off the track, Rick has never asked for special consideration or asked for a competitive advantage."[18]

But it is what Bill France did next that so poignantly and powerfully symbolizes the NASCAR spirit. France organized a program to raise money for leukemia victims and to recruit bone marrow donors. To help with the effort he rounded up a shining list of some of NASCAR's finest: drivers Jeff Gordon, Terry Labonte, Ricky Craven, Darrell Waltrip, Dale Earnhardt, Ken Schrader, Bill Elliott, and Rusty Wallace; team owners Roger Penske, Joe Gibbs, and Felix Sabates.

The Racing Against Leukemia Marrow Drive was launched at the 1997 Daytona 500. All three Hendrick drivers display the 1-800-Marrow-2 sticker inside their cars where onboard cameras broadcast the phone number for millions of television viewers. In less than five months, NASCAR fans have made 20,000 phone calls to the hotline. Three donor matches had been made by late summer, including one between a fifteen-year-old girl and a member of the Hendrick Motorsports No. 25 Budweiser team.

Whatever the decision of the federal court in Asheville or the greater trial in the fight for his life, one thing is clear. Rick Hendrick is a class act. He is admired by his employees, respected by his competitors, and forever a loved member of the NASCAR family.

8

THUNDER ROAD INTO
THE NEXT CENTURY

THE 3,300 FANS piled into Brasington Grandstand at Darlington Raceway have been waiting almost an hour for the race to begin. The TranSouth Financial 400, the spring race at Darlington, is not quite as famous as the Southern 500 but it *is* a Winston Cup race and it always gets the fans excited.

Named after the track's founder, Brasington Grandstand is the smallest and the oldest structure left at Darlington. It still has the original wooden-plank floor and tin roof. At one point, the entire frontstretch at Darlington was one long porch that kept the fans shaded from the hot South Carolina sun. But over the years, windstorms and hurricanes have ripped away sections of the grandstand roof and seats—all except Brasington, which stubbornly hangs on to its past. Although its seats are not the best in the house, it does have the advantage of placing the fan closest to the action, for the grandstand sits right against the wall of the infamous turn four.

For Brasington Grandstand, this particular Sunday is extra special. After today's race, the track is going to flip-flop. To accommodate the track's expansion plans, the start–finish line will be placed in front of the new Tyler Tower across from us starting with the Mountain Dew Southern 500 in September 1997. At that point, the frontstretch where I am sitting will become the backstretch. Today will be the last time Brasington Grandstand will host turn four.

The fans around me are more than ready. Their headsets and scanners are in place, tuned to the frequency of their favorite team. They have cheered the drivers' introduction and then stood respectfully for the national anthem. Now they are itching for the race to start.

Finally, the announcer ignites the crowd with the four most famous words in motorsports: "Gentlemen, start your engines." A huge roar from the fans engulfs the track but is soon drowned by the thunder of forty-two race cars firing their 700-horsepower engines. The thunderstorm moves slowly out of pit row.

Over the past year, as I have studied the business of NASCAR, I have come to realize that the economic engine in this sport is every bit as powerful as the thunder that is now shaking the wooden floor of Brasington Grandstand. Anyone who still thinks of NASCAR racing as a quaint sport for good ol' boys is in for a monumental surprise.

Even more remarkable is the phenomenal surge of growth in recent years. In the 1990s NASCAR Winston Cup racing has exploded with double-digit growth. It is an economic pace we normally associate with the early stages of a business lifecycle. Yet even though NASCAR is fifty years old, this business is showing no signs of slowing down. We need only a quick review of attendance numbers, track expansion, and television ratings to see that NASCAR is an economic force to be reckoned with.

Between 1990 and 1996, attendance at NASCAR's Winston Cup series grew an astonishing 65 percent. During this same period, NBA attendance increased 17 percent, NFL 6 percent, and Major League Baseball 5.8 percent.

Track owners can't build capacity fast enough to keep up with the demand. Tracks that already have Winston Cup dates are adding seats at a blistering pace, and several new tracks are patiently waiting for their first Winston Cup event.

In 1997 alone, Daytona International Speedway added another 18,000 seats and built 24 new hospitality suites. Richmond is currently building 12,000 new seats; Phoenix will add another 25,000. Darlington is building the 7,800-seat Pearson Tower, named for David Pearson, the track's winningest driver, along turn two. Bristol Motor Speedway is expanding to 131,000 seats and adding 75 more luxury suites. Dover Downs International Speedway has just announced a plan to add 73,000 seats. By the year 2004, Dover will own 170,000 grandstand seats and 65 corporate suites. Roger Penske's California Speedway, after one year in operation, is building 30,000 more seats; by the year 2003 it will have a total of 200,000 grandstand seats—twice as large as the Rose Bowl.

New state-of-the-art racetracks have been built in southern California, Dallas, Miami, and Las Vegas. The ultramodern Las Vegas Speedway, with 100,000 seats and 102 skyboxes, has already been awarded a new Winston Cup date. The new Homestead Complex in Miami, jointly owned by Penske Motorsports and International Speedway, hopes it will get a Winston Cup race.

Even without a race date in their pocket, track owners are planning new facilities, gambling on NASCAR's future. Penske Motorsports has taken an option on 640 acres of land adjoining the new Denver airport. There is speculation that by 1999, a new two-mile superspeedway with 105,000 seats could be ready for a Winston

Cup date. International Speedway Corporation is also taking a very serious look at the Kansas City market. The facility would be a 1.5-mile oval track with 75,000 seats (expandable to 150,000). By adding tracks in Denver and Kansas City, NASCAR continues to fill in the locations of major markets where it currently does not have a Winston Cup date.

The television audience has also expanded at a phenomenal rate. Halfway through the 1997 season, ratings at ABC and CBS were up an average 20 percent compared to 1996; cable ratings had improved 25 percent.

Daytona International Speedway is adding lights to the racetrack. The 1998 Pepsi 400 will be run in the evening on July 4, and the race will be telecast in prime time on CBS.

In the 1998 season NASCAR will expand the Winston Cup season to thirty-three races. The new race will be at the Las Vegas Speedway, a new market for stock car television. According to Neal Pilson, president of Pilson Communications, the television rights for this race are starting at $4 million, and there is strong interest from ABC, ESPN, and TNN.

Early in the race, Darlington has lived up to its reputation: The track too tough to tame is collecting drivers left and right. In the first fifty-eight laps there are six caution periods as a result of wrecks strewn across the track. Dale Jarrett, who won the pole, led early, but at the midway point it's Jeff Gordon on the lead lap.

At about lap 150, I make my way from Brasington Grandstand over to the Darlington Room, the raceway's own hospitality suite. Jim Hunter, president of Darlington Raceway, holds a reserved seat and caters lunch for the many special guests who attend the race. The suite seats 114, and for every race at Darlington, it is packed full. NASCAR executives, corporate sponsors, team owners, some of the brass from ESPN, and South Carolina's top politicians, including congressmen, senators, and Governor David Beasley, are among those who accept guest invitations.

The atmosphere inside the Darlington Room is companionably electric, with smiles and congratulations all around. The TranSouth Financial is another great event. Darlington has never looked better, and NASCAR has never been stronger. But no one is dwelling on the success of the day. Rather, the buzz in the room is about what is to come and how NASCAR is going to reach the next level.

Future Growth

In one sense, the arenas for growth in NASCAR are obvious: still greater expansion of tracks to accommodate rising attendance, ever higher television ratings. But what makes the NASCAR economic model so compelling is that, even if those two elements were to level off, the organization could still grow at a double-digit rate. How? By leveraging the opportunities available in three areas whose potential has been only barely tapped: sponsorship, licensing, and technology.

Sponsorship

For most of its history, the NASCAR organization has stayed behind the scenes and has allowed drivers, teams, and tracks to attract and negotiate their own sponsorship deals. But if NASCAR is going to continue to grow financially, sponsors must continue to get a solid return on their investment. For every dollar they put into NASCAR, there must be a corresponding increase in sales.

NASCAR has found a powerful way to increase sponsors' return and at the same time create a stronger financial foundation for drivers, teams, and tracks: integrated marketing. By putting its considerable influence and expertise behind a carefully managed program of integrated marketing that will enable sponsors to leverage all of the resources available, NASCAR is taking a proactive role in moving the concept of sponsorship to a much higher level.

The first step is to create the opportunity for drivers, teams, and tracks to work with a sponsor. Functioning somewhat like a facilitator, NASCAR management will actively set up linkages between companies interested in becoming sponsors and teams, tracks, and drivers interested in new sponsorship opportunities. What NASCAR hopes to do is broaden the sponsors' thinking by showing them how to assemble a multipronged approach that involves not just one driver or one race but a far more powerful coordinated package.

The next step is to activate the integrated sponsorship. The most common activator is media exposure: television, radio, print, and online advertising. That exposure is then carried all the way down the line to the point of sale, where shelf hangers, floor displays, countertop signs, and special packaging prominently display NASCAR's connection with the product.

Sponsors are quickly learning that activating a NASCAR integrated sponsorship not only generates more sales but also allows for more creative ways to get their message across to consumers. One case in point is Anheuser-Busch.

In the past few years, sales of canned beer have declined about 10 percent compared to bottled beer. Anheuser-Busch wanted to reverse this trend, and targeted its Busch brand for a special campaign using NASCAR's integrated sponsorship program. The strategy was to use a popular driver and familiar racetracks to promote special commemorative cans. Dale Earnhardt starred in a series of commercials that profiled colorful tracks, including Darlington and

Bristol. Since the introduction of the program, sales of Busch beer in cans have grown 7 percent—a seventeen-point swing from the competition.

NASCAR is so confident of the value of its integrated approach that it plans to develop racing-related themes for combined marketing impact. Each year, the entire sport will be focused on one overall theme, providing sponsors an integrated, coordinated platform for their marketing messages. The first platform is the 50th Anniversary celebration in 1998. The year-long celebration will be divided into quarters, each with a particular theme. Sponsors involved with the anniversary celebration will coordinate their marketing promotion around each theme. The strategy is being executed perfectly by The McIlhenny Company, makers of the world's best-known hot sauce, Tabasco.

Starting in 1998, Tabasco will become the primary sponsor for the NASCAR Winston Cup No. 35 team owned by International Sports Management. The team will race Pontiacs driven by Todd Bodine. It is McIlhenny's first major commitment to sports marketing, but already the company is acting like a seasoned NASCAR sponsor. Tabasco will become an "Official Marketing Partner" of the 50th Anniversary celebration, and will be a featured participant in the quarterly marketing programs. The company itself will develop special promotions that relate to the quarterly themes, will aggressively advertise on television, and will produce point-of-purchase displays that tie into the quarterly promotions.

No doubt about it, the anniversary celebration will be a grand year-long party. It takes nothing away from the success of fifty years to also use the occasion for a concentrated marketing program. Mark Johnson, president of PRIMEDIA, a sports marketing firm that developed the anniversary strategy, commented, "This is the perfect opportunity to celebrate the rich heritage of NASCAR, while allowing the fans and sponsors to participate in the sport all 365 days of the year."[1]

Licensing

Like sponsorship, the licensing program in NASCAR is designed to benefit drivers, teams, and tracks by growing business opportunities for the sport's corporate partners. Companies have learned that putting the NASCAR name on their product increases their retail presence, and for that they are happy to pay a licensing fee. But NASCAR believes that there is room for enormous expansion in this area, to the benefit of all parties.

So, to help create a stronger foundation, NASCAR has taken the lead in promoting licensing arrangements. The first step has been to expand consumer awareness of NASCAR beyond its traditional market by finding a way to reach people who have never attended a race. That was the marketing purpose behind establishing NASCAR Thunder, the official store of NASCAR, and NASCAR Café. To date there are ten NASCAR Thunder stores in shopping malls around the country. The first NASCAR Café opened in March 1997 in Myrtle Beach, South Carolina; the next two are set to open in Nashville and Orlando—the most popular tourist destinations east of the Mississippi.

For years, the sale of NASCAR souvenirs occurred mostly at trackside trailers and small retail shops. But no more. Today, Wal-Mart, Kmart, Toys "R" Us, J.C. Penney, and Sears have all begun purchasing NASCAR apparel and toys for their shoppers.

NASCAR's newest licensing program, and potentially the strongest of all, is designed for the automobile aftermarket. The public sees NASCAR as a reputable motorsports organization that upholds the highest standards; in one recent market survey, 91 percent of the consumers and retailers polled said they would favor a product with the NASCAR name attached.[2] Drawing on that reputation, NASCAR is in a position to offer its corporate partners a very strong opportunity to distinguish their brands in a very crowded marketplace. But that opportunity comes with one condition: Before NASCAR will endorse any automotive product, the company must first sponsor a driver, team, or track.

The benefit for these corporate partners is twofold. Not only do they get to use the NASCAR name in conjunction with their product, they also have the opportunity to participate in the new integrated media program called NASCAR Garage. NASCAR Garage is a television program, a radio show, two publications, and a section on NASCAR Online devoted to automobile repair and maintenance.

Already several well-known consumer companies have signed up: Unocal, Quaker State, Wix oil filters, and Raybestos. But the early winner in this unique relationship appears to be Exide Batteries.

Exide Batteries sponsors the No. 99 team at Jack Roush Racing and also sponsors the fall race at Richmond International Raceway, known as the Exide Select Batteries 400. The company recently became a NASCAR-licensed provider of batteries and backed this commitment with a $15 million advertising campaign, including television commercials featuring its role as "the official battery of NASCAR." Was it worth the investment? Overall, battery sales in the automobile aftermarket have declined by 10 percent—except for Exide, which has seen sales *increase* 20 percent.

The thinking behind NASCAR's sponsorship and licensing programs has helped to elevate the financial strength of this sport both for its participants and its corporate partners. These new strategies form a foundation that will help support NASCAR at a time when the rate of growth in attendance and television ratings will inevitably slow. But one additional business opportunity still remains for NASCAR, and its potential is overwhelming.

Technology

The mission statement for combining NASCAR and technology is straightforward. "Use technology to bring the fan closer to the sport," said Bill France Jr. The first step in bringing that mission statement to reality was NASCAR's Website, NASCAR Online, an established success. Coming up immediately behind it is a level of fan interaction that no other sport can match. Indeed, it is technology that sets NASCAR racing apart from every other sport.

From its inception three years ago, NASCAR Online has been devoted to fulfilling the wants and desires of race fans. Today, www.nascar.com is one of the most popular Websites, with over 500,000 weekly users and 22 million hits a week.

NASCAR Online provides race fans with all the information they could want: the latest NASCAR news and race results; background information on each driver, team, and track; a chat room for fans; and a multimedia section that allows online users to listen to interviews and watch film footage of race highlights. Click on one icon and you move to the NASCAR Garage; click another and you're at the NASCAR Store, where you can buy the latest souvenirs.

NASCAR Online has evolved rapidly. Today, you can go online during a race and have access to the same information that is available to NASCAR officials, including driver positions and weather radar. Paul Brooks, NASCAR's director of special projects, who oversees new technologies, says, "We are constantly searching for ways to develop new technology that will bring the fan closer to the sport. The next step will be putting web cams in the garage area so fans can see what goes on behind the scenes; next we'll probably have them at the drivers' meeting and on the inspection line. We always ask ourselves, what would the fans want next?"[3]

So what do NASCAR fans want? To drive in a race, what else? With NASCAR Racing 2, a CD computer game, fans can race at virtually all NASCAR tracks, including Talladega, Charlotte, and Darlington. When he first saw the product, Bill France Jr. commented that there should be a way for friends in different locations to race against one another. That led to the development of the Racing Online Series. In this Internet racing league, online drivers will participate in the same way a NASCAR Winston Cup team does, including setting up the race car, pulling in for pit stops, and then racing other competitors for the checkered flag. There will be online rule books and NASCAR officials who will sanction championship races.

Before long, race fans with a home computer can enjoy the ultimate thrill: competing in a real race, in real time. Technology that can instantaneously feed the positional rankings of each driver into the computer already exists. What is needed next is a link between the cars on the track and the image that occurs on the home computer, and that solution is not far off. Imagine going head to head with Jeff Gordon at the Daytona 500 for three hours; short of actually driving a race car, you can't get any closer than this.

It is the potential of this technology that differentiates NASCAR from other sports. Right now, you can play simulated basketball games on a computer, but you can't pit your skill directly against Michael Jordan. With NASCAR, you can put your own driving skills on the line; your reflexes, your nerve, your ability to handle the car, all go into the computer competition, right along with the NASCAR drivers.

What makes online racing so intriguing is the need, and the opportunity, for sponsors to advertise at the computer races. "After all," said Paul Brooks, "our sport is not authentic without the sponsors."

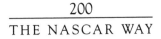
There is no end to what technology can do for NASCAR; there is practically no end to the marketing opportunities that new technology will create for NASCAR sponsors.

It is easy to see why everyone in the Darlington Room is optimistic. While other sports are struggling not to lose ground, NASCAR clearly is ready to soar.

What is the ultimate source of this growth? As a business analyst trying to pin this down, I found that practically everyone associated with NASCAR has an opinion. Some claim the growth is a result of the new star system that profiles charismatic drivers like Jeff Gordon and Dale Earnhardt. Others will tell you the breakthrough came in 1994, when NASCAR stormed into Indianapolis Motor Speedway for the first stock car race on the track that is synonymous with Indy-style racing, and sold out all 265,000 seats. A few claim NASCAR saw a direct benefit when baseball turned its back on its fans. An increasing number of people believe that NASCAR's growth is due to the marketing efforts of Brian France and his team.

All of these statements are valid. However, as I search for the one fact that is most responsible for NASCAR's success, it would have to be that the sport has finally reached critical mass. With increased fan attendance and television viewership, coupled with the millions of dollars dedicated to sponsorship, licensing, and marketing, NASCAR has finally reached a level where the sport cannot be overlooked. It has become too big to ignore, and now is being carried forward by its own momentum of success.

The NASCAR Way

In the Darlington Room are some of the most influential members of the NASCAR family, with roots in the sport going back to the earliest days. Some of them, mindful of the stereotypes about the South and the sport of stock car racing, find it pleasantly ironic that, over the past five years, NASCAR racing has exploded out of its regional constraints and captured the attention of the whole country.

All those screaming fans in Delaware, New York, New Hampshire, California, and Indiana are, I believe, telling us something. They are telling us that the underlying ideals that are embodied in NASCAR mean something to them too. You don't have to be from the South to understand and appreciate the NASCAR way of doing things.

The NASCAR Way is a collection of attitudes, values, and ideals. Those values are put into action every day, in the way NASCAR does business. At rock bottom, then, the NASCAR Way is a business model, and like any model, it has a few guiding principles waiting to be uncovered and understood.

The only legitimate way to analyze a business is to look at it in the context of the industry of which it is a part. So we start by comparing NASCAR to its competitors, in the industry called sports entertainment.

The phenomenal success of the NASCAR organization rests largely on the fact that its financial house is in order. The sport has three primary revenue providers: race fans, sponsors, and television networks. The genius of NASCAR lies in this financial structure. All three elements are strikingly in balance, supporting NASCAR like a solid three-legged stool. This means that no one revenue provider carries the load at the expense of the other two. The implications of that apparently simple observation are enormous.

Think for a moment about the other professional sports organizations. Professional football, basketball, and baseball all receive revenues from fans, sponsors, and television just like NASCAR. But over the past several years, the greatest amount of revenue for stick-and-ball sports has come from television rights, at the expense of fans and sponsors. Now that television rights provide the major funding for these sports, there is less incentive to repay fans and sponsors for their investment. We have already seen what that kind of disincentive has done for those sports.

NASCAR, on the other hand, knows that its fans and sponsors are the financial underpinning of the sport. To date, television rights, although rising in value, do not contribute nearly enough to support NASCAR. Just as it has from the beginning, NASCAR depends on fans and sponsors for its very survival. Because these relationships are interlocked, NASCAR cannot afford to ignore one revenue provider for another. It is this very stable financial design that has enabled NASCAR to zoom forward.

Every entertainment sports business has observed the surging popularity of NASCAR, and all of them are now double-checking their business plans.

But replicating NASCAR's success may require more than just rebuilding relationships with fans and supporting sponsors. A deeper analysis reveals there is something more profound here than just selling sports entertainment. It can be argued that NASCAR thrives because it operates in an environment of unbridled capitalism. NASCAR has become an example of the capitalist model working at its best. It is a sport that is still built on opportunities, not guarantees.

Racetracks, unlike fields, arenas, and ballparks, are not built by taxpayers and government guarantees. Rather, they are built by investors with capital at risk; to get a return on their investment, they must rely on fans to buy tickets. Remember, the sanctioning agreement between NASCAR and the track owner lasts for only one year; the implication is that a renewal is based on performance.

Race teams are not guaranteed franchises that retain their value regardless of performance. They are business opportunities made possible by corporate sponsors. These corporations expect performance and will assuredly withdraw their sponsorship if performance is lacking. The value of any NASCAR race team is directly proportional to its level of success.

Drivers are not guaranteed enormous salaries just for showing up. Unlike other professional athletes, who receive the same salary whether their team loses or wins in any given game or season, drivers are compensated for winning races. Without long-term contracts negotiated in advance, drivers earn their income by performing well during the season and by showering appreciation on their fans, who return the admiration by purchasing licensed products.

When compensation is paid regardless of performance, there is a tendency to get mediocre results. NASCAR works because compensation for all its participants—track owners, teams, and drivers—is tied to results.

Of course Big Bill France did not set out to create an exercise in capitalism or any other political-economic theory. He wanted to build a sound business based on a sport he loved. A capitalist model creates better results, but it is not free of abuse. Over time, the market will weed out underperformers, but to ensure fair play, each system needs a governing body. NASCAR is no different. NASCAR has succeeded because it has the right financial design and because it has been able to operate in a capitalist free-market system. But the brilliance of NASCAR is being seen, more and more, as the brilliance of an extremely well run family business. There are lessons here for all types of businesses.

To begin with, NASCAR has the right product. Exciting door-to-door racing using Detroit fixtures has proven to be a hit with fans. Big Bill France's instincts were exactly right. Stock car racing is number one in motorsports, completely outrunning Indy-style racing, which tends to promote less competitive races using cars that few fans can identify with.

The second important element that NASCAR does right is nothing but common sense, but NASCAR does it at a level of sheer genius: Love your customer. The profit system in NASCAR is possible only with the help of its fans. If getting a return on your investment requires you to treat respectfully the people who make your business flourish, then that's what you do. When your money is at stake, your attitude is markedly different.

It is important to have the right product and it is necessary to have the right business design. But for any company to succeed for fifty years, it must also have the right management.

When you speak of NASCAR management, you are speaking of the France family; their personal traits are the same as the values that drive the company: fair-minded, honest, unquestioned integrity, smart, open-minded, flexible. Fifty years of success is their validation.

In modern economic times, the businesses that have provided the greatest return for investors have been those that were structured with opportunities, not guarantees. What NASCAR is doing is not revolutionary; it is actually rather old-fashioned: Respect your customer, have the right product, organize the financial rewards so that everyone benefits. That's the NASCAR Way.

I decided to watch the last of the race from the Media Center, directly above the Darlington Room. It's not as plush as the suite below, but there is plenty of room for reporters to spread out and type on their laptop computers. A bank of telephones stretches across the back wall, next to a high-speed copy machine.

Many reporters in this room have written about NASCAR for years. Bob Latford and Tom Higgins have followed the sport longer than some younger reporters have been alive. But young and old alike, they all have one thing in common: They are die-hards who take their job seriously and who write passionately about the sport they love.

With twenty laps remaining in the TranSouth Financial, Dale Jarrett is close to winning the race. Many of the reporters are secretly pulling for Dale because of what happened the last time he ran on this track, in last year's Southern 500. Racing for the million-dollar bonus, Dale's No. 88 Ford Thunderbird hit an oil patch and slammed into turn three, ending any chance of winning the Winston million.

Now, with just a few laps to go, Dale is holding a slim lead over Ted Musgrave, driving the No. 16 Family Channel Ford for Roush Racing. On the last lap, Ted and Dale are bumper to bumper. Ted tries to pass but Dale manages to hold on, finally crossing the finish line 0.169 seconds ahead of Ted. It is a special win for Dale Jarrett; his father, Ned Jarrett, won at this track in 1965.

Sitting high above the track gives me an opportunity to scan Darlington Raceway. Down below, Dale Jarrett and the Quality Care Ford team pose for pictures in victory lane, quickly changing hats so each picture will profile a different sponsor. To my right, the fans in Tyler Tower are beginning to file out. The campers and pickup trucks in the infield are packing up. The world's greatest traffic jam is about to begin.

Looking down at the track one last time, I think about the very first race at Darlington. The day Harold Brasington's dream came true. The day Big Bill France sanctioned and organized what was then the largest race in NASCAR's history. The day Bill Jr. sold snow cones in the infield.

With reporters in the media center clicking away on their computers, e-mailing stories to their editors, I also think about Frankie Patterson, the sports editor from Kannapolis who attended the first race at Darlington and who banged his story out on a manual typewriter with a single light bulb hanging above. Frankie too looked out at the track that day and wondered whether all those people would ever come back to Darlington.

They did come back, Frankie. They came back by the millions, and they brought their money.

EPILOGUE

NASCAR, like the stock cars that circle the track, is in constant motion. There is never a shortage of racing news. Teams that win bask in the media spotlight; teams that lose begin the "silly season" shuffle. On the business side, the news is also fast and furious. Here are a few recent developments that I believe warrant your attention:

- On June 20, 1997, tobacco executives and state attorneys-general reached a temporary settlement on the major lawsuit against the industry. Among the provisions was a ban on tobacco advertising and sponsorship of sporting events. The immediate concern for racing was the effect this would have on NASCAR, because of the longtime sponsorship of R.J. Reynolds and its Winston cigarette brand. It now seems clear that NASCAR will not be harmed by this announcement.

  The current agreement, which is subject to both congressional and presidential approval, does not take effect until December 31, 1998. In the event the agreement stands, one of two possible outcomes seems likely. First, R.J. Reynolds could maintain its involvement by switching its advertising and sponsorship to one of its many other non-tobacco consumer products. Second, NASCAR could enter into a sponsorship agreement with a new non-tobacco company. In either case, the number of multibillion-dollar corporations that have shown interest in becoming a NASCAR sponsor invites the possibility that there may be more suitors than available series sponsorships.

- The newest NASCAR Winston Cup race, bringing the series to thirty-three races, will be held at the new Las Vegas Motor Speedway on March 1, 1998. Tickets for the event went on sale September 22, 1997; all 100,000 were sold out in thirty hours.

- Ford Motor Company announced that the Ford Taurus, America's best-selling automobile, will become the company's NASCAR Winston Cup series car beginning in 1998. The Ford Thunderbird, after winning 176 Winston Cup races, 5 Daytona 500s, 2 drivers' championships, and 2 manufacturers' championships, will be retired at the end of the 1997 season.

- As of October 1997, Washington Erving Motorsports had yet to announce a Winston Cup team for the 1998 season. Its Busch Grand National team will be driven by Jimmy Foster and sponsored by Dr. Pepper.

- Also for the 1998 season, Jack Roush has expanded his multi-car operation to five Winston Cup teams. Chad Little and Johnny Benson join Mark Martin, Ted Musgrave, and Jeff Burton as Roush Racing drivers.

- In 1996, Dale Jarrett came within one race of winning the Winston $1 million bonus. In 1997, Jeff Gordon went all the way. Like Dale, he won the Daytona 500 and the Coca-Cola 600 at Charlotte, and then Jeff went on to win the Mountain

Dew Southern 500 at Darlington, making him the first driver since Awesome Bill Elliott in 1985 to win the Winston Million. He immediately donated $100,000 of it to the National Marrow Donor Program in Rick Hendrick's honor.

- On August 14, 1997, Rick Hendrick pleaded guilty to mail fraud as part of an agreement that settled the fifteen-count federal indictment against him. Government prosecutors recommended a $250,000 fine and ten to sixteen months' confinement, to be served at Rick's home.

This decision to settle was not easy for Rick Hendrick, but he was left with little choice. Since February 1997, Rick has endured daily injections of the drug alpha-interferon to combat his leukemia. The side effects from this drug are physically debilitating. To have the strength to properly defend himself, Rick would have had to cut back on the medication—a decision that might have killed him. In the end he made the only choice possible: to fight the greater fight.

Meanwhile, the bone marrow donor drive is picking up steam all across the country. Kellogg's recently announced that it is publicizing the 800 hotline number on 42 million cereal boxes. Revell will donate $150,000 from sales of a special gold-plated die-cast car to the marrow campaign. Special donor drives, in which potential donors are typed and added to the data bank, have been held in Charlotte, Fayetteville, and High Point, NC; in Richmond and Martinsville, VA; in Indianapolis; in Brooklyn, MI; and Bristol, TN. More than 12,000 people have been typed. Through fundraisers and donations, more than $400,000 has been contributed to the Marrow Foundation in Rick Hendrick's name. "I hope everyone understands this is not for me," Hendrick said. "It's for the 3,000 people looking for a donor, their only hope for survival.

I'd trade both of my Winston Cup championships for one life-saving match."

- On November 21, 1996, Elmo Langley died while driving the pace car in Suzuka, Japan. Elmo, along with the entire NASCAR contingent, was in Japan to run the Thunder Special 100 exhibition race. While giving Buddy Baker a quick tour of the track, Elmo suffered a massive heart attack. Baker knocked the car out of gear and steered it to the side of the track. Later he recalled the smile that stretched across Elmo's face as he let out his last sigh.

  Elmo Langley was one heck of a driver. Before radios, cool suits, and power steering, Elmo was muscling stock cars around tracks throughout the South. He started in 532 NASCAR races, finished in the top five 63 times, and won twice: at Spartanburg Fairgrounds and Old Dominion Speedway, both in 1966.

  Even today, I can remember Elmo's smile. He shared it with me more than a few times that hot September afternoon at Darlington Raceway. Sitting in the pace car, between caution laps, Elmo told me countless stories of the great NASCAR drivers of yesterday as well as the great ones circling the track that day. Although I was new to racing, Elmo quickly made me feel a part of the NASCAR family. It was a day I will never forget.

  So long, Elmo. Thanks for the ride.

NOTES

Chapter 1   Riding with Elmo

1. Mike Hembree, "Flagging an End of an Era," 1997 TranSouth Financial's official program, p. 42.

Chapter 2   Rules of the Road

1. Tom Wolfe, "The Last American Hero Is Junior Johnson—Yes!" *Esquire* (October 1965), p. 211.

2. Peter Golenbock, *American Zoom—Stock Car Racing from the Dirt Tracks to Daytona* (New York: Macmillan, 1993).

3. "The Nascar Story" video series, vol. 1, "The Early Years" (ESPN Home Video, Creative Sports Inc., 1993).

4. Goodyear Tire & Rubber Company special report, referenced in *Winston Cup Scene,* March 1997.

Chapter 3   It Takes Money to Race

1. Greg Fielden, *Forty Years of Stock Car Racing, vol. 1: The Beginning, 1949–1958* (Surfside Beach, SC: The Galfield Press, 1992), p. 43.

2. Interview, Bill Schmidt, vice president for marketing, Gatorade Worldwide, March 4, 1997.

3. Nanette Byrnes, "Rolling Billboards," *Financial World*, April 12, 1994.

4. "Top Ten Sponsorship Myths We Wish Would Go Away," *IEG Sponsorship Report*, January 16, 1995.

5. Byrnes, "Rolling Billboards," p. 48.

6. John Helyar, "Can Baseball Get Sponsors Back to the Ballgame?" *The Wall Street Journal*, November 15, 1996, p. B1.

7. David Greising, "The Race around the FDA," *Business Week*, September 9, 1990.

8. Interview, Shelley Morrison, executive vice president, Starwave Corporation, February 21, 1997.

9. Martha M. Hamilton, "Races Start Engines and NASCAR Sponsorship Zooms," *The Washington Post*, May 26, 1996, p. 1.

10. Steve Ballard, "Gordon Helps DuPont Stay on Track," *USA Today*, July 3, 1996, p. 10c.

11. Interview, Paul Brooks, July 10, 1997.

12. *Winston Cup Illustrated*, December 1996, p. 66.

Chapter 4   Prime Time

1. Interview, Neal Pilson, Pilson Communications, January 21, 1997.

2. James Tuite, "Petty Wins Daytona After Leaders Crash," *The New York Times*, February 19, 1979, p. C1.

3. Tuite, "Petty Wins."

4. Fielden, *Forty Years of Stock Car Racing*, vol. 4: *The Modern Era, 1972–1989*, p. 253.

5. Interview, John Wildhack, senior vice president for programming, ESPN, March 7, 1997.

6. Michael Hiestand, "Big Picture: Many Factors Create Decline," *USA Today*, January 28, 1997, p. C1.

7. Interview, Rudy Martzke, reporter for *USA Today*, March 9, 1997.

8. "ISC Inks Deal with CBS, ESPN," *Winston Cup Scene*, October 3, 1996, p. 66.

9. "CBS on the Daytona 500," *NASCAR Quarterly*, February 1997, p. 1.

10. "Gaylord Announces Merger of Cable Network Operations with Westinghouse/CBS," Gaylord Entertainment press release for Wall Street Analysts.

11. *NASCAR Quarterly*, February 1997.

12. Interview, Wayne Harris, WNPC-FM, Newport, TN, March 12, 1997.

13. Interview, Dale Jones, WNPC-FM, Litchfield, CT, March 12, 1997.

14. Interview, Chris Wallace, WDSD-FM, Dover, DE, March 12, 1997.

15. Interview, Tom Higgins, *NASCAR Winston Cup Scene*, March 14, 1997.

16. Interview, Steve Ballard, *USA Today*, March 11, 1997.

17. Interview, John Griffin, NASCAR director of communications, March 23, 1997.

18. Interview, Dave Mingy, *Sports Illustrated*, March 11, 1997.

19. Interview, Stephen Madden, *Sports Illustrated*, March 11, 1997.

Chapter 5 The Meanest Mile

1. Jim Hunter, *A History of Darlington Raceway and the Joe Weatherly Stock Car Museum* (Columbia, SC: Branyon Publishing, 1968), p. 5.

2. Hunter, *History*, p. 5.

3. Hunter, *History*, p. 5.

4. Hunter, *History*, p. 7.

5. Hunter, *History*, p. 7.

6. Hunter, *History*, p. 9.

7. Hunter, *History*, p. 13.

8. Hunter, *History*, p. 13.

9. Hunter, *History*, p. 16.

10. Fielden, *Forty Years of Stock Car Racing, vol. 2: The Superspeedway Era*, p. 51.

11. Fielden, *Forty Years*, p. 51.

12. Fielden, *Forty Years*, p. 11.

13. Fielden, *Forty Years*, p. 11.

14. Fielden, *Forty Years*, p. 11.

15. Bo Cheadle, analyst, Montgomery Securities Motorsports Conference (New York, March 20, 1997).

16. Interview, Rick Horrow, May 7, 1997.

17. Taylor Damonte and Tom Regan, *Market Analysis of Selected Visitors Segments in Florence and the Pee Dee Region* (Columbia: Institute for Tourism, University of South Carolina, June 1996).

18. Interview, Lesa France Kennedy, January 7, 1997.

Chapter 6 True American Heroes

1. Interview, Tom Higgins, May 21, 1997.

2. *NASCAR Winston Cup Scene*, April 24, 1997, p. 45.

3. Golenbock, *American Zoom*, p. 331.

4. *Becket Racing Heroes: Dale Earnhardt* (Dallas: Becket Publications, 1995), pp. 21, 31.

5. "Is Earnhardt the Greatest Driver? Our Panel of Experts Say, You Bet He Is," *Inside NASCAR* (January/February 1997), p. 31.

6. Randall Lane and Peter Siegel, "The Year of the Michaels," *Forbes* (December 16, 1996), p. 244.

7. Robin Hartaford, "Collectibles and Souvenirs," *Stock Car Racing* (November 1996), p. 96.

8. Interview, Doug Rose, May 22, 1997.

9. Interview, Don Hawk, president of Dale Earnhardt, Incorporated, March 22, 1997.

10. Bill Fleischman, "Hot Wheels," *Philadelphia Daily News*, July 16, 1996, p. 72.

11. *Stock Car Racing*, March 1972.

Chapter 7 Forty-Two Teams on the Same Field at the Same Time

1. Larry Fielden, *Tim Flock: Race Driver* (Pinehurst, NC: The Galfield Press, 1991), p. 127.

2. "The NASCAR Story," video series, vol. 1.

3. "The NASCAR Story."

4. Bones Bourcier, "Why Hendrick Wins," *Stock Car Racing*, January 1997, pp. 20–22.

5. Bourcier, "Why Hendrick Wins."

6. Bourcier, "Why Hendrick Wins."

7. Thomas Pope, "Going in House," *NASCAR Winston Cup Scene*, October 10, 1996.

8. Interview, Jimmy Johnson, March 20, 1997.

9. Beth Tuschack, "Elliott: I was history when Hendrick drivers hooked up," *USA Today*, February 18, 1997, p. 2C.

10. Tuschack, "Elliott."

11. Bones Bourcier, "Ray Evernham—Lucky Man? Hardly!" *Stock Car Racing*, June 1996.

12. Ben White, "The Crew Chief," *NASCAR Winston Cup Illustrated*, March 1997.

13. Ed Hinton, "Strength in Numbers," *Sports Illustrated* Presents 1997 Season Preview, p. 1118.

14. Hinton, "Strength in Numbers."

15. Interview, Joe Washington, July 3, 1997.

16. *NASCAR Winston Cup Scene*, May 29, 1997. p. 10.

17. Pete Schnatz, "Erving Revving Up a NASCAR Team," *Philadelphia Inquirer,* July 19, 1997, p. C1.

18. NASCAR corporate statement, December 9, 1996.

Chapter 8 Thunder Road into the Next Century

1. Interview, Mark Johnson, president of PRIMEDIA, July 11, 1997.

2. Poll conducted by Interbrand Schechter, a New York branding agency, cited in Matthew Conner, "NASCAR: A Symbol of Quality, Performance," *NASCAR News,* October 23, 1996, p. 1.

3. Interview, Paul Brooks, director of special projects, NASCAR, July 10, 1997.

INDEX